ALL IS WELL
IN THE
GREAT MESS

AN ADAPTATION OF THE INNER CHAPTERS
OF THE *ZHUANGZI*
WITH REFLECTIONS

SCOTT P. BRADLEY

Published by BookLocker.com, Inc., Bradenton, Florida, U.S.A.

Printed on acid-free paper.

BookLocker.com, Inc.
2015

First Edition

DISCLAIMER

This book details the author's personal experiences with and opinions about the philosophy of Zhuangzi. The author is not licensed to speak for Zhuangzi.

The author and publisher are providing this book and its contents on an "as is" basis and make no representations or warranties of any kind with respect to this book or its contents. The author and publisher disclaim all such representations and warranties, including for example warranties of merchantability and/or advice for a particular purpose. In addition, the author and publisher do not represent or warrant that the information accessible via this book is accurate, complete or current.

The statements made about products and services have not been evaluated by the U.S. government. Please consult with your own legal or accounting professional regarding the suggestions and recommendations made in this book.

Except as specifically stated in this book, neither the author or publisher, nor any authors, contributors, or other representatives will be liable for damages arising out of or in connection with the use of this book. This is a comprehensive limitation of liability that applies to all damages of any kind, including (without limitation) compensatory; direct, indirect or consequential damages; loss of data, income or profit; loss of or damage to property and claims of third parties.

You understand that this book is not intended as a substitute for consultation with a licensed medical, legal or accounting professional. Before you begin any change your lifestyle in any way, you will consult a licensed professional to ensure that you are doing what's best for your situation.

This book provides content related to philosophical topics. As such, use of this book implies your acceptance of this disclaimer.

A REVIEW OF THIS BOOK

Scott Bradley reads, lives and breathes the spirit of Zhuangzi with his blood—not to mention with his eyes and his ears as they open into the world, with his knowing consciousness as it plumbs and unravels both its other and itself, and with all the cells in his body: he reads the Zhuangzi as Zhuangzi tells us the Genuine Person breathes: from his heels.

A bystander can only sigh in gratitude to see that this is still possible, heartened that the pulse of Zhuangzi finds its channel in the world yet: in his many years sailing the watery part of the world—the Daoiest part of the Dao, according to some—led only by the radiance of drift and doubt, Bradley has floated his craft safely past both the Scylla of know-nothing New Age enthusiasm and the Charybdis of scholarly forestblind literalism, past both theomorphic piety and complacent humanism, producing a highly accessible, spirited and subtle interpretative rendering and evocation of the Zhuangzi which at the same time communicates the living spirit and the lifeblood of its argument with a rigor and attention to crucial nuances and distinctions which is heartbreakingly lacking in most works on the subject. Bradley's work makes sense of the Zhuangzi, and rides that sense true and close, all the way out to the refreshing life-giving open sea of its sense-preserving senselessness.

Brook Ziporyn
Professor of Chinese Religion, Philosophy, and Comparative Thought
The University of Chicago Divinity School

"Who can free himself from achievement

And fame, descend and be lost

Amid the masses of men?

He will flow like Dao, unseen.

He will go about like life itself,

With no name and no home.

(Thomas Merton; *The Way of Chuang Tzu*)

CONTENTS

INTRODUCTION

This book is a criminal enterprise. When an author makes every effort to be as ambiguous as possible, carefully covering his tracks with layer upon layer of doubt inspiring ruses—who has the right to attempt a clarification of his message? But have I not just done so? Zhuangzi is such an author, and in saying so, I have clarified his message. What is that? That life is inherently ambiguous and cannot be clarified. The crime has already been committed. Still, did he not have more to say than that we-cannot-know-anything-for-sure? He did. Yet never did he stray from this foundational insight, but rather made it the point of departure for his every remedial response to the tenuous reality of the human experience. In digging here, beneath all this profound ambiguity, we should not, therefore, believe that we will have uncovered hidden 'truths'—that would be the true crime.

Yet, still another crime has been committed here nonetheless. For I have taken Zhuangzi's text and given it my own interpretive (and manipulative) spin. Admittedly, this spin is an honest attempt to clarify what Zhuangzi had to say in response to his discovery of the limits of all saying, but in personalizing and particularizing it in this way I have robbed it of some of its ability to inspire the same personalized response in others. The reader is thus encouraged to seek out other, more 'precise' renderings, as well. Only let the reader remember that these too have their own unavoidable interpretive spins. Zhuangzi nods his head and gives us an encouraging smile.

My first encounter with Zhuangzi came through the agency of Thomas Merton's *The Way of Chuang Tzu* (1969), a not-always-true-to-the-text adaptation of Zhuangzi that hooked me for life. To this day, portions of that adaptation continue to inspire me as the more literal and 'correct' renderings have failed to do. I offer this snippet of personal anecdotal history as justification for this project you now have in hand.

There is a spirit to Zhuangzi. No mere scholarly rendering of his words can capture that spirit; nor can one render them well without a sense of that spirit. Merton realized some of that spirit and was thereby better able to share Zhuangzi through his 'misreadings' than some have done in their precision. Again, Zhuangzi himself smiles broadly.

None of this is intended to denigrate the work of scholars. Without them there would be no Zhuangzi with whom the rest of us could play. To you scholars, then, I now thankfully light a stick of joss. Only I would also remind you and the reader that there is somewhere Zhuangzi suggests we might enjoy going, and that that journey is not facilitated by excessive concern over the meaning of this word or that, or whether Zhuangzi was the author of any of what, for convenience, we take to be his work. This, too, is allowing the spirit of Zhuangzi to guide the interpretive process.

Implied in all this is my belief that I have here captured something of the spirit of Zhuangzi. I cannot deny it; why else would I have published it? Nevertheless, I also understand that, in the spirit of Zhuangzi, neither this nor any other representation of his philosophy could possibly be a final word, and indeed, that no representation, to the extent that it arises from genuine heart-felt engagement, could be anything but 'correct' and affirmable.

ZHUANGZI AND THE BOOK THAT BEARS HIS NAME

What little is thought to be known about Zhuangzi (Chuang Tzu) (ca. 369-286 B.C.E.) is this: He was a minor official working in a place known as the Lacquer Grove in the state of Meng. That's it. As for the book that bears his name, he is thought by most scholars to be the author of only the first seven of its thirty-three chapters of our received version, though it is possible that some of his work might also be embedded in some of the other chapters. Some question whether he wrote any of it. Such 'facts' are hotly debated by scholars, but they need not concern us. What difference does it make? It is only for the sake of convenience that I take Zhuangzi to be the author of the first seven chapters, known as the Inner Chapters. These chapters, whoever their author, evince a unified vision and seem to be the work of one hand, and again for convenience sake, I take them as such. As for the rest, several widely divergent schools of thought are represented, one of which might be labelled "School of Zhuangzi". These latter, though they demonstrate deep sympathy with the philosophy of Zhuangzi, also frequently diverge from him in areas of fundamental importance and are thus not always the best lens through which to clarify his thought. For this reason, this present work deals almost exclusively with the Inner Chapters.

Our received version of the *Zhuangzi* comes to us courtesy of Guo Xiang (252-312 C.E.) who whittled it down from the fifty-two chapters he received. What other editing he might have done we do not know. Might he have re-titled and re-arranged these Inner Chapters? We do not know. In addition to his editing, he also wrote the first extant commentary on it, and we shall have opportunity to share some of his insights in what follows. Some have accused him of having plagiarized substantial parts of this commentary from Xiang Xiu (ca. 227-272), one of the "Seven Sages of the Bamboo Grove". Again, for our purposes, so what?

It is hoped that in relating some of the profound questions that revolve around the *Zhuangzi* the reader will come to realize the importance of de-mythologizing both Zhuangzi and his ostensible writings. Were Zhuangzi himself here to instruct us, he would likely entreat us to do so. This is one man's personal response to the contingencies of his life as experienced, not a holy text, and definitely not a revelation of eternal truths. In the end, origins, authorship, and antiquity have no relevance whatsoever (beyond establishing an interpretive context) to the realization of its suggested outcomes. To all these aforementioned difficulties we might add textual variations and, most importantly, the cultural and personal biases of those who have translated it for us. Like everything else in life, this document is, in the words of Zhuangzi, "strangely un-fixed", and that is just how he would have it. We serve its message best when we take it as such.

PHILOSOPHICAL DAOISM

Even the use of the designation "Daoist" to describe the philosophies of Zhuangzi and his contemporaries and forebears of similar persuasion is widely debated among scholars. Since these were only lumped together as a "school" two centuries after their passing, this is understandable. Yet, though they did not see themselves as members of this school, or any other, to be sure, it hardly matters that in retrospect we see them as precursors of this school and label them as such. We might call them proto-Daoists, but this amounts to the same thing. Once again, for convenience, I will occasionally call Zhuangzi a Daoist, but more frequently a philosophical Daoist.

This latter designation is similarly not without its controversy, and this, to my thinking, is where names start to matter. The problem is that "Daoism" covers as broad range of thought and orientations, and when discussing Zhuangzi it becomes important to identify how he differs from most of them. Present day Daoism is essentially religious; it has its church, its beliefs and doctrines, its saints and 'immortals'. This bears no resemblance whatsoever to the philosophy of Zhuangzi, though 'his' book has been dutifully added to its canon, and he himself inducted into its pantheon. Though religious Daoism can legitimately trace its roots back to *before* Zhuangzi, I take this as demonstrating how his philosophy was in fact a counter-response to it, rather than contiguous with it.

Some parts of the anthology known as the *Guanzi* likely pre-date Zhuangzi's Inner Chapters, and though they make use of similar terminology, they express 'positive teachings' that not only do not appear in Zhuangzi, but seem to be consciously countered by him. The most important of these are the beliefs that though metaphysical Dao is unknowable, one can still 'attain' it, and that *qi* (vital force) can be cultivated so as to achieve some form of a higher state of existence. These, in my view, are essentially religious aspirations which I understand as completely antithetical to Zhuangzi's understanding of the human experience and his suggested response to it. For this reason, I am careful to identify Zhuangzi's philosophy as "philosophical Daoism" in contrast to religious Daoism, and when speaking of Daoism have this in mind. This, at any rate, is my clear bias—Zhuangzi was not the proponent of a religious remedy to the problems inherent to the human experience, but rather eschewed all positive teachings about 'spiritual' realities *as* a central aspect of his suggested remedy. The philosophy of Zhuangzi, in my view, does not lend itself to the essentially religious aspirations of the plethora of New Age remedies, but rather offers a viable, non-religious alternative to them.

NO SAGES NEED APPLY

Was Zhuangzi a great sage? Has there ever been any such a one as a sage? How could we possibly know? And why would we require one, in any case? I pose these questions with a view to revealing the extent to which we tend to default to religious—that is, absolutist—solutions to so-called 'spiritual' matters. If there were never any sages—fully realized human beings—what belief system could we follow with any assurance that it was true and effective? Who could we follow? Rather than following supposed sages, Zhuangzi tells us, "We would do much better to follow and evolve along our own daos" (6:8/10). So, let's do the same with Zhuangzi—let's allow him to be one who only aspired to an elusive freedom, just as we do. Zhuangzi had no need for sages because he had no need to believe in a final 'solution' to the unfixed, "dangling" character of the human experience. Rather than negating this existential given, he turned it into the means by which to playfully wander within it. Our tenuous predicament is never resolved, but ever-exposed and illuminated so as to render it ever-useful.

But he often speaks of sages, one might protest. Indeed he does. One subsists on only wind and dew and flies on the backs of dragons. Another hangs out with the Creator of Things. Yes, and gigantic fish transform into vast birds; trees, birds, cicadas, centipedes and snakes speak; and shadows debate with their own shadows. Why would we wish to select out from among these fantastic and playful stories some that are deadly serious? To do so would be to efface Zhuangzi's entire project.

We will have occasion to refer to the final chapter of the *Zhuangzi* (the 33rd) where the philosophies of many of Zhuangzi's contemporaries and predecessors are presented and critiqued. I mention it here to point out the curious habit we see within it of assuming that those who advocated for a way of being in the world actually realized it. We are told, for instance, that "Shen Dao abandoned cleverness, rid himself of any personal position, and instead followed along with whatever was unavoidable. . . . Moving only when pushed, proceeding only when pulled, he was like a twirl in the breeze, like a spinning feather . . . making no mistakes . . . free from blame" (Ziporyn 2009; p 122). Surely, *he* must have been a sage! But no, the author tells us, he did not know Dao. Then why, we might ask, did the author suggest that he had realized that to which he could have only aspired? Similarly, why would we need to believe that Zhuangzi had fully realized that to which he aspired? Only if, in fleeing doubt, we needed to believe in fast and sure answers—but these are precisely what Zhuangzi eschews at every turn.

WHAT MOTIVATES THIS WORK

This is not a scholarly work—a fact no doubt already abundantly clear to the reader. Instead, it is a very personal response to the philosophy of Zhuangzi as part of the process of developing a personal philosophy of life. Though every effort has been made to faithfully interpret Zhuangzi's philosophy, it is unavoidable that my biases have also had a large part in the process. Its value to the reader, should there be any, lays primarily in its being just such an engagement; the actual interpretative conclusions are only secondary. Thus, though I cannot help but believe that Zhuangzi as I have understood him has much of value to offer to the unfolding of other philosophical pilgrimages, the reader is encouraged to engage with him so as to develop her or his own interpretation of him.

One might justifiably ask what an obscure philosopher from the 4th Century B.C.E. has to offer someone of our time seeking to develop her or his own philosophy of life. In reply, we answer that Zhuangzi's thought is in many ways amazingly relevant in its response to the awakening to the limitations of faith, language and reason that has also typified our own age. Contemporary philosophy deals with precisely these same limitations. Existentialism, for instance, asks in the absence of all faith in things religious and the failure of reason to fill that void, how we can best live, and in the case of some expressions, why we should bother to live at all. To this author's thinking and experience, these profound existential problems persist. Zhuangzi asks and answers these same questions.

His times, described as the Warring States Period, were turbulent. With the fall of the Zhou Dynasty, along with its institutions, the world was thrown into chaos. Not coincidentally, this was also the time of the Hundred Philosophers, a fertile moment in which a multitude of voices spoke in an attempt to bring order back to the world. Zhuangzi was but one of those voices.

Still, the question remains, Why Zhuangzi? We reply first that, in harmony with the very thought of Zhuangzi, it need not be Zhuangzi. We are invited to "choose our own piping"(1:6); there being no final definitive 'answer' to the question of how best to live, we are free to grow our own using those resources that seem best to inform our unique journeys. This author has found Zhuangzi to be just such a resource. Perhaps the reader will find his thought similarly helpful.

This book consists of three elements presented in two parts. In Part One I have paraphrased and adapted much of the text of the Inner Chapters. After each chapter I then reflect upon its message. So as to allow the reader an uninterrupted experience of the text, though I have divided it into parts, the corresponding reflections are left to the end of each chapter. In Part Two, I briefly present something of my own philosophy of life as it presently stands. I call this The Simple Way since, in the end, it simply affirms all things as they are in every present moment. All is well in the Great Mess.

In the case of this new rendering of the Inner Chapters, because it has greatly clarified their message for me, I cannot help but think that it might do the same for others. This rendering is not strictly speaking a new translation since it has used the English translations of others as its template. The translations consulted will be found in the bibliography. However, I should make special mention of Brook Ziporyn's *Zhuangzi: The Essential Writings with Selections from Traditional Commentaries* (Hackett: 2009) since I have found this work the most helpful and frequently quote both from his translation outside the Inner Chapters and from the portions of the commentaries he has made available.

For considerations of space and in avoidance of redundancy, I have omitted some of the text. Centered ellipses indicate where an entire vignette has been omitted. Ellipses aligned left indicate where a portion of a vignette has been omitted. I have also arranged the text into numbered verses to facilitate easy reference to the text.

PART ONE

ADAPTED TEXT AND REFLECTIONS

CHAPTER ONE
WANDERING FREE IN NON-DEPENDENCE

THE TEXT—PART ONE

WANDERING FAR AND UNFETTERED

1 A vast fish named Not-Yet-Really-a Fish (Kun) dwells in the Mystery-of-Pre-Existence (the Northern Oblivion). This fish transforms into Existence as a vast bird named Just-Like-You (Peng). This bird must wait upon the yearly monsoon and then, with a great effort ascends ninety thousand miles to make its Flight-of-Existence to the Mystery-of-Post-Existence (the Southern Oblivion).

2 All this is found in *The Equalizing Jokebook*.

3 Is blue the sky's true color? Looking up, we do not know. Peng flies so high that when he looks down he also sees only blue without knowing why.

4 A big bird requires a lot of wind to get aloft and goes far. A small bird requires little wind to get aloft and goes only a short distance. Yet are they not in many ways the same?

5 But the cicada and tiny dove scoff and laugh at Peng for going so high and far and believe that their short glides are the best and only reasonable way to fly.

6 It's very difficult for a small awareness to understand the experience of a large awareness. Consider the morning mushroom; it knows nothing of noon. Or consider the cicada that is born and dies in winter; what can it know of the other seasons? Yet there are trees that live for millennia and a man named Pengzu who lived for hundreds of years. We think that some

live short lives and others long lives, but such distinctions are only relative to our species determined perspective. We would love to live as long as Pengzu, but the trees would laugh at us for the pettiness of our ambition. Is there a sense in which long duration and short duration are the same?

THE TEXT—PART TWO

7 Human beings typically think just like the cicada and tiny dove. They take their small accomplishments as meaningfully fulfilling their lives and scoff at the idea of being free of both 'meaning' and 'fulfilment'. They slave away at trying 'to be somebody'.

8 Some, like my good friend Huizi who became prime minister of Liang, think that the opinion of others—that they are 'great and successful men'—suffices to make them 'somebody'. They depend on the external.

9 But even the philosopher Song Xing would laugh at them. Song understood that the opinion of others could not fulfil one's need to be 'somebody' and instead focused on the internal, on self-respect. If the whole world praised or condemned him, it would not concern him. He also said that an insult could not bother us if we were 'somebody' by our own reckoning. But does this truly suffice to make us 'somebody', or do we still need to strive?

10 Some, like Liezi, pursue 'spiritual' achievement in an attempt to be 'somebody'. He was so 'spiritual' that he could 'ride the wind' for fifteen days before coming back. But still he depended on the wind—and isn't this just emblematic of his continued dependence on the need to be 'somebody', even if a 'spiritually advanced' somebody?

11 But what if you depended on nothing at all? Imagine that. What if you just charioted upon whatever seems true of the cosmos and upon everything and anything that happens? How could your soaring ever be brought to a halt?

12 That's why I say that the person with the vastest possible human awareness—let's call her a 'sage'—has no need to "be somebody" at all—she has no-fixed-identity—and thus no need to accomplish great deeds or to be esteemed by others.

TEXT—PART THREE

13 Now, when the mythical sage-emperor Yao realized that the sage Xu You brought prosperity to his Empire without actually doing anything, he asked if he wouldn't take over the Empire from him. "It's stupid to keep the torches burning when the day has come or to water the fields when it's raining," he said. But Xu You replied, "Since the Empire is already prospering, why would I want to *do* something? Only if I wanted 'to be somebody'; but to need to be somebody is to be as dependent as a guest. The tailorbird calls the vast forest home, but is content to nest on a single branch. The mole has an entire river at his disposal, but only drinks a belly-full. I have my role and you have yours—so keep your Empire."

14 Now, Jian Wu related to Lian Shu the words of the madman Jieyu who spoke of having an awareness vast like the cosmos—words that Jian found completely ridiculous and impossible for human beings to realize. Lian wanted to know what he could possibly have said!

15 Jian replied, "He said there is a seemingly ageless sage, living on a holy mountain while subsisting on only wind and dew, riding the wind, and hitching his chariot to dragons so as to wander beyond the known world. He said this sage concentrates his spirit and all things flourish. Personally, I think this is a lot of ridiculous 'big talk' and can't believe it."

16 "Of course you can't!" replied Lian Shu. "Blindness is not only a physical malady. If you were to believe it, in any case, that would be like a virgin pretending to know all about love-making. This sage has no need to be known or believed. He lets the world sort out its own mess, and all things flourish; why would he want to impose himself upon it?"

17 "And not only that, nothing could ever harm such a man. Floods could not drown him; scorching heat could not burn him. Having no fixed-self, what would he have that could be drowned, burnt or lost? From his leavings you could make mythical sage-emperors like Yao and Shun, though he would think nothing of them."

18 "It's like the salesman from Song who took ceremonial caps to sell to the barbarians in the north when they had neither need nor desire for such things. Why would a sage wish to impose himself on others?"

18 "Or, it's like Yao who, after imposing order upon his Empire, went to see four sages on that same holy mountain and was so amazed that he forgot all about his Empire."

19 All of this reminds me of my friend Huizi. The King of Wei gave him the seed of a gourd which, when he had grown it, weighed more than a hundred pounds. Unable to think out of the box, he found it too big to use. First, he tried to store water in it, but it was too heavy to lift. Then, he cut it in half to use as a dipper, but it was too big to fit into another container. "It was big to be sure," he said, "but because it was useless I smashed it to bits."

20 He was referring to my 'big words', of course—just like the dove scoffing at Peng's high flying or Jian's rejection of the words of Jieyu. So, I told him he just wasn't able to see the usefulness of things outside the conventional ideas of usefulness. I told him the story of some silk dyers from Song who had invented a wonderful balm to protect their hands in their winter labors. When a stranger heard of it, he bought it, used it to win a winter sea battle, and was given his own fiefdom. The dyers were bound by convention and slaved away throughout the winter, but the stranger who could think outside the box became a lord.

21 Instead of smashing it to bits, I told him, he could have made it into a boat in which to float about happy and carefree on the rivers and lakes. This is where 'big words' can take you! But Huizi's mind was all tangled up by worldly ideas of success.

22 Another time, Huizi told me about his big, useless Stink Tree. It was so gnarled and twisted that nothing could be made from it and no carpenter would give it a second glance. "And your words are just as big and useless," he said. "That's why everyone rejects them!" They do? No matter.

23 So, again I tried to show him how usefulness is largely a matter of perspective, and how conventional ideas of usefulness can often lead you into bondage. Take for example a weasel. It's really good at catching mice, being incredibly nimble and athletic. But that same leaping athleticism ends up getting it caught in a net. The lumbering yak, on the other hand, is completely useless when it comes to catching mice, but its very bigness insures it will never be caught in a net! So, I told him, why not take your big, useless tree and plant it in the village-of-no-need-to-be-anyone in the vast-fields-of-nowhere-in-particular? "Then you could wander far and unfettered beside it, take a nap beneath it, and do lots of useless nothing together with it!"

24 The Stink Tree, moreover, because of its supposed uselessness will never be cut down. Might not Huizi's life, if he can similarly learn to be useless, be preserved and flourish?

REFLECTIONS—PART ONE

FAR AND CAREFREE WANDERING

There are numerous facets through which to peer into the heart of Zhuangzi's essentially mystical vision. There are his logical arguments of which some suggest an intellectual framework by which to imagine a sense of the oneness of all things. Others demonstrate the limits of the reasoning mind so as to invite us to experience life in a more immediate and less mediated way. Another suggests the possibility of the loss of one's very sense of being a definite and fixed self so as to facilitate an experience of oneness. There are 'skill stories' that advocate realizing a sense of self- and world-transcendence through full 'spiritual' absorption into the work at hand. Meditative techniques for achieving an empty openness seem, on occasion, to be suggested. The manner of one's orientation toward the endless procession of events, especially those deemed unavoidable, is often offered as a means to transcendence. All of these and more are presented as both descriptions of a mystical possibility and as a means to its realization. These descriptions and means are, however, in many ways subsumed by these presented here in this first chapter. For a description of this mystical experience we have *xiaoyaoyou*, 'far and carefree wandering'. For a means to the realization of that wandering we have depending on nothing, or, as I choose to call it, non-dependence.

Unlike the titles for the other chapters of the *Zhuangzi*, which simply take a word, phrase or name from the opening sentence, those of the Inner Chapters are clearly intended to summarize the contents of the chapters they represent. This suggests that they may have been assigned at the time of their original compilation, while those of the other chapters suggest a later addition for the sole purpose of providing a convenient handle. In any case, it clearly behooves us to examine these titles of the Inner Chapters as integral parts of the text itself.

Thus, we begin with the title of chapter one, *xiaoyaoyou*, far and carefree wandering. If this is indeed descriptive of Zhuangzi's ultimate mystical vision, then, for all its intriguing and inviting qualities, it still strikes us as surprisingly this-worldly and mundane. And so, in a very real sense, it is; for Zhuangzi recognized no relevant Ultimate Reality with which to engage or unite, and no cosmic rift in need of redemptive or salvific mending. It is only this world here in which we have our existence that concerned him. And thus his sole aspiration lay in discovering how best to live, how to flourish in our humanity, in the context of this world-experience and its givens. As for the 'rest', it is among the givens of the human experience that this must forever remain unknowable, requires no identification to be what it is, and in any case enfolds us all in a vast and affirming oneness.

Zhuangzi's actual description of this experience in the chapter now under consideration is spare. It emerges only as we engage with the many stories, parables, anecdotes, dialogs and monologues in the text ahead of us. It is our engagement that elucidates this vision for us, and this, only as we begin to experience it and make it our own. For this reason, we would do best here to let the meaning of far and carefree wandering reveal itself as we work our way through the text.

The suggestion of the possibility of living in the attitude of non-dependence that makes this wandering possible is, on the other hand, clearly detailed in this chapter, as we shall see. Non-dependence is not in-dependence; for it recognizes that all transient beings are by their very nature utterly dependent on each other and upon the mysterious source of their arising. Rather, it is an attitude of release in trust into that very dependence. It is an attitude of trust in that it fears no loss no matter what happens. Where all things form 'one body', no singular, individuated body is ever at risk. This is not a guarantee of the perpetuation of a specific identity, but the realization that the fear consequent to the possible loss of individual identity reveals that clinging to our present identity is a source of disharmony, and that our integration into the whole does not require any identity at all. Non-dependence is thus revealed as a release from all fear—ultimately, nothing can harm us, for whatever happens, all is an expression of the Great Happening. All is well in the Great Mess.

THE FLIGHT OF EXISTENCE

Zhuangzi begins with a fantastic myth. This sets the stage for all that follows both in terms of content and methodological tone. In the case of the latter, we are immediately alerted to the playful quality of Zhuangzi's entire project. None of this should be taken as a presentation of fixed truths which, if unacknowledged or not adhered to, will lead to dire consequences. Take it or leave it; it will not affect ultimate outcomes. Seriousness is the gravest enemy of the serious. Playfulness is an attribute of wandering; to take anything too seriously would be to bring our wandering to a halt.

If we had any doubt about this playful tone, Zhuangzi dispels it by telling us that his myth comes from a book called *The Equalizing Jokebook*

(Ziporyn's translation and admittedly only one of several possible renderings). It is doubtful that any such book existed, and likely that his readers were immediately aware of this fact. He probably made it up. It is itself a joke, and an invitation to not only not take this myth or the points it makes as anything more than a playful suggestion of a possible response to the human experience, but also to not take all that follows as such. Perhaps Zhuangzi wanted us to take this as the title of *his* book. In any case, he never stops inviting us to laugh.

I have taken great liberty in presenting this myth so as to express my primary interpretation of it. The myth itself has many levels of interpretive possibility, and I have chosen that which I think is its primary message, though this will not hinder us from exploring its other possibilities.

We see a vast bird, Peng, arising from one unknowable Oblivion only to fly to another. This represents the actual existential circumstance of everything extant, whether it be a rock, a tree, a human being, or likely, the universe. Thus, I call this the flight of existence. There is, however, something apparently unique about the human experience of this flight of existence, namely that we are aware of ourselves making it, and this leads to our concern that it ends as it began, in complete, unfathomable mystery. When all is said and done, this is Zhuangzi's central concern—how do we make the most of our self-aware existence in the context of its suspension in utter mystery? We might, in a moment of glib rationalism, be tempted to ask what the problem is, but we know in our hearts that the unavoidable fact that our flight will come to an end in death colors the entirety of our life experience. Zhuangzi suggests that, typically, death negatively impacts everyone's life experience, admits that it certainly does his own, and leaves any deniers to their denial. It is the fear of death and pall it throws over life that most concerns Zhuangzi.

This flight ends as it begins, in Oblivion. There are two iterations of the myth given, though I have omitted the second. In the first, the destination, the Southern Oblivion, is called The Pool of Heaven. In the second iteration, it is the Northern Oblivion of origin that is called the Pool of Heaven. They are the same. We are inclined to ask to where we are going, but it seems just as valid to ask from whence we have come. Since both equally represent unfathomable mystery, no true distinction can be made between them. There is, however, a case to be made for the prioritization of the mystery of origin since it lies behind us as that which might have given us answers were it possible to do so. The fact that it does not informs our present existence. For this reason, in the *Zhuangzi* and later in Zen we are enjoined to consider what we were before our mothers and fathers were born. Whatever that 'was' or, more to the point, was not, tells us something about what we presently take ourselves to be. And though Zhuangzi, at least, would not go so far as to answer 'nothing', he does think this speaks to the fallacy of the belief that our sense of identity is anything more than a 'temporary lodging'. Thus, Yan Hui, after the discovery of his own inner emptiness, declares his realization that "'I' have never even begun to exist" (4:12). Thus, the myth of the flight of Peng invites us to seriously consider the implications of our suspension in mystery to our very sense of being a discrete self-identity.

THE TRANSFORMATION OF IDENTITY

Before Peng was Peng 'he' was Kun; before 'he' was a bird 'he' was a fish. There is no telling what 'he' might become next. This is a crucial aspect of Zhuangzi's advocacy for our psychological uniting with the apparently ceaseless transformation that is the cosmos. The concept of reincarnation, the transmigration of 'souls', which also appeals to a sense of a continued participation in the ever-changing, also typically implies a perpetuation of some form of identity. 'I' take a new form, but the 'I' persists. This is not the view of Zhuangzi. For him, what is important is not that the form changes, but that the very identity transforms from one identity to another. No discreet 'I' is thought to continue. Not only is this view much more radical, and immediately less assuring, it is also much more difficult to express. Kun does not become Peng; whatever of Kun there is in Peng is empty of a Kun-identity. In a later chapter, when someone speaks of what 'he' will become after death—perhaps a rooster or a bug's arm—we are required to keep this distinction in mind. The problem arises from the nature of language itself; words signify an identity, and it is therefore near impossible to speak of one thing becoming something else without that seemingly implying a continuity of some form of identity.

Perhaps we can get a better sense of this when we realize that the name for Kun, whom Zhuangzi identifies as a vast fish, actually means fish roe. Thus, I have named him "Not-Yet-Really-a- Fish". He is in some sense simply the mere possibility of a fish while simultaneously the vastest fish imaginable. An actual identity, in his case, is already in doubt. We are reminded of Yan's discovery that his self-identity has not yet begun to exist. Kun represents this inexplicable being-without-a-fixed-identity.

For his part, Peng's compound name, in addition to referring to a vast mythical bird, the Chinese version of the Phoenix, also designates him as a 'peer' or 'friend'. Vast and exceptional as he is, we are all still his equal. Thus, I have called him "Just-Like-You".

SIZE DOESN'T MATTER

With this we can shift to the presentation of Peng in the context of the tiny birds and cicada that scoff at his great effort to ascend to ninety thousand miles to make his flight of existence—they make their own flights with much less drama. Clearly we are intended to recognize the greatness of Peng in contrast to the pettiness of these scoffers. Zhuangzi immediately uses this to illustrate the relative differences in perspective between a large consciousness and a small one, and later, in the second chapter, advocates for the former over the latter. These are two distinct points of view regarding the big and the small; one demonstrates that sense in which they can be taken as different but also the same, while the other demonstrates how they are not equal. These two points of view taken together represent an essential principle at work in most all Zhuangzi's philosophy, namely, the realization of a third, 'higher' point of view that is able to embrace both the equality of all things and their inequality. He calls this "Walking Two Roads". This allows us to simultaneously affirm all things just as they are while also seeking their improvement. Once we understand that things are perfect by virtue of their being perfectly what they are, we can work to make them better.

The tiny bird and cicada, because they scoff and consider their manner of flight "the best and only reasonable way to fly" (1:5), can be judged as having "a closed-awareness bound to a fixed-self [that] is narrow and insular" (2:7). However, this is only implied here. Instead, Zhuangzi frames their differences from Peng in terms of their relative and unavoidable (innate) limitations. The mushroom that grows and dies in a single morning cannot possibly conceive of the afternoon—nor should we expect it to do so. The cicada is born and dies in the winter; would it not be an example of a closed and narrow awareness to judge it as inferior because it doesn't understand the other seasons? The tiny birds are in error because they scoff, not because they are unable to match Peng's incredible flight. Were their responses reversed with Peng scoffing at the feeble flight of the birds, while the birds affirmed both their own and Peng's flights in recognition of the fulfillment of their respective capabilities, then it would be Peng who demonstrated a small consciousness and the birds a large one. Size doesn't matter; it is the fulfillment of one's capabilities within one's limits that matters. Yet, here again we are required to apply "Two Roads"; if the tiny birds scoff, then their scoffing in some sense demonstrates their limitations—can we reasonably expect them to do otherwise? At best all we can do is be the occasion, provide the space, for them to realize another possibility.

Guo Xiang (252-312), the editor of our received *Zhuangzi*, and author of its first extant commentary, states this 'higher' point of view succinctly: "Though some are larger and some are smaller, every being without exception is released into the range of its own spontaneous attainments, so that each being relies on its own innate character, each deed exactly matching its own capabilities. Since each fits perfectly into precisely the position it occupies, all are equally far-reaching and unfettered. How could any one be superior to any other" (Ziporyn 2009; p 129)?

VASTER AWARENESS IS NOT MORE KNOWLEDGE

Zhuangzi uses the blue of the sky when we look up to emphasize the incredible height of Peng's ascent—he is so high that he too only sees blue when he looks down. But Zhuangzi also asks why the sky is blue at all. And thus, since Peng also sees only blue, we are informed that despite the grandness of his achievement, despite the largeness of his awareness, still this simple mystery remains unsolved. This is critical to understanding Zhuangzi's mystical vision. A vast awareness is not one that has solved life's mysteries, but rather one that has taken full advantage of them to facilitate a greater openness. It is our not-knowing that occasions our open release into the omnipresent Mystery. No new knowledge is acquired thereby. No final understanding is realized. No 'true purpose' is discovered. All remains just as it has always been—inexplicable Mystery.

This is the usefulness of the useless, a theme we shall explore shortly. It also provides a glimpse of Zhuangzi's extraordinary appreciation of the value of our limitations. Never are we enjoined to strive to overcome our innate limitations. Rather, we are encouraged to discover them so as to make the fullest use of them—the more we have and the more we discover the better! We transcend when we fully embrace that over which we transcend. We fly and soar when, like Peng, we have discovered sufficient air resistance to ascend to incredible heights. Without resistance, without obstacles, no transcendence is possible. Very real limits are our only means to a realization of a sense of limitlessness.

ZHUANGZI AS PENG

Finally, we should not overlook Zhuangzi's very personal reasons for framing this myth as he has; he seems to be writing especially to his friend and chief foil, the "logician" Huizi. Indeed, the entire book may very well have been written with Huizi in mind. Some have conjectured that Zhuangzi was once a disciple of Huizi, for he does indeed echo his critique of reason in the second chapter, and makes frequent reference to him throughout. But he has gone beyond his teacher in exploring the implications of the limits of "the understanding consciousness", and here playfully takes his friend to task. Thus the myth can be seen as a reply to the criticisms of Huizi, where Zhuangzi is Peng and Huizi is a relatively tiny creature of small consciousness. It seems to echo a supposed encounter between them related in the 17th chapter. Huizi has become the prime minister of the state of Liang and hearing that Zhuangzi is coming, fears that he might attempt to usurp his position. After evading attempts to intercept him, Zhuangzi appears of his own accord and scoffs at the idea that he would seek anything so worthless as worldly power: "In the south there is a bird called 'Yuanchu'—have you heard about it? This bird rises from the Southern Sea and flies to the Northern Sea, resting only on the sterculia tree, eating only the fruit of the bamboo, and drinking only from the sweetest springs. An owl who had found a rotten mouse carcass saw Yuanchu passing overhead and screeched, 'Shoo! Shoo!' Now you—are you trying to shoo me away from your state of Liang" (Ziporyn 2009; p. 76)?

Such an interpretation is further supported in the closing anecdotes of this first chapter where Huizi criticizes Zhuangzi's philosophy as "big but useless", very much like the scoffing of the cicada and tiny birds at the fantastic flight of Peng.

The significance of this personal side to these Inner Chapters is twofold. On the one hand, we learn that understanding Huizi contributes to our understanding of Zhuangzi. On the other hand, we realize that his philosophy did not arise in a vacuum, but was rather a product of his engagement with not only Huizi, but also many others of his relative contemporaries. Without Huizi there would likely have been no Zhuangzi. If this seems to relativize and de-mystify that philosophy, so much the better; the way of Zhuangzi is not *the* Way, but rather just another very personal response to life in a particular context. Whatever use to which we put that response, therefore, should similarly be in response to our own unique contexts.

REFLECTIONS—PART TWO

BEYOND THE NEED TO 'BE SOMEBODY'

We typically dwell within tiny, self-contained bubbles and view the world from that perspective alone—just like the tiny birds and cicada who scoff at Peng's flight because it is so different from their own. We needn't see this as a moral issue—doesn't every individuated being on the planet do the same? They do. Everything and everyone ultimately sees things from its own perspective and looks after its own interests; this is how they and we survive. In the case of us humans, however, the reality of our self-awareness and the knowledge of our impending death lead to a deep-rooted sense of disharmony within our bubbles. This is a practical problem, not a moral one. We 'have' a self. And 'having' a self, we fear its loss. This is our greatest fear. But there are other fears as well. If this self were sufficient unto itself, if it stood firm and complete within itself, then we might still fear its possible extinction in death, but at least we would not fear its daily diminution. But we do. This self upon which we lean, it turns out, is a flimsy reed indeed. Though we are sure that it truly exists, it never seems to completely agree with us. It's like a hologram that requires us to ceaselessly turn the crank that provides the current that energizes it. It must forever prove to itself and others that it is full and real. It believes itself to 'be someone' yet paradoxically must continually struggle to be that someone. But is not this fixed 'someone' simply a story we have made up? Zhuangzi believes it manifests as such.

Sartre describes human existence, "being-for-itself", as "a being such that it is what it is not and is not what it is". This speaks to the reality that we are more a becoming than a being. But we needn't fully understand what this is intended to convey in order to get a sense of the tenuous character of the human experience it identifies. Nor do we need Sartre—nor Zhuangzi, for that matter—to describe it for us; only a moment of genuine self-inquiry suffices to demonstrate that our self does not and cannot stand on its own; it requires our continuous efforts to prop it up. The entirety of Zhuangzi's philosophical project can be seen as an attempt to free us from this exhausting labor and the fears that inspire it.

Not surprisingly, we humans think of ourselves as special in a world where we alone seem to be fully conscious of ourselves as selves. And in a very real sense, we are. Yet, it is also the case that in a very real sense we are not special. We seem to be simultaneously of Nature and yet not of it. There are Two Roads at play here as well—two apparently contradictory yet simultaneously arising perspectives—we are both uniquely transcendent of Nature and mundanely the same. The sense of self is something that has arisen in Nature's unfolding just like everything else. It is, for all practical purposes, accidental. And like everything in Nature, it presents as something temporary and experimental—wonderful, but somehow flawed; the experiment may become so successful as to endure for a 'long' while. Or, it may not. It will, in any case, have its end like everything else. In this context of an awareness of its own temporality, humanity can be relieved of some of the burden of its own sacrosanct self-importance; we can understand how we are not special. We can also understand how that we might be inherently dysfunctional. Out of Nature self-consciousness arose, and out of that a sense of self. Proto-humans left the safety of the trees, started to walk upright on two legs, and became prone to bad backs. Humanity evolved self-consciousness, developed a sense of self, and became internally dualistic and disharmonious. This is the price of admission, the price we must pay for self-awareness. There are exercises and techniques for alleviating the problems arising from having weak backs, and the same for the problem of internal disharmony. Again, this is a practical issue, not a moral one.

Zhuangzi was not plagued by the cultural imposition of a belief in a fixed and immortal human 'soul'. Thus, he was able to address the experience of self with what for us is a fresh sense of realism. He was, in this sense, very much a phenomenologist. He did not see it as his task to explore what the self actually 'is'—that would be "to use what the understanding knows to delve into what it cannot know" (6:1). Rather, he simply explored how it manifests; and since it manifests in part as dysfunctional, he sought how to practically remedy that problem. Why? Because life itself wishes to flourish, and human flourishing involves its own self-enjoyment. His remedy does not, therefore, seek to "add something to the process of life", but rather to let life fulfil itself.

In light of this, we can see why Zhuangzi never advocates for the discovery of one's 'true self' (or 'essential self', or in a latter iteration, 'buddha-nature'), as if there existed some fixed and real self behind or beyond our dysfunctional selves. There is (in actual experience) only this self we now have and with which we can perhaps tinker so as to make it work better in the delivery of our enjoyment of life. The pursuit of some idealized self would be to add to the process of life and would overturn

17

Zhuangzi's project at the onset. The point is not to realize some idealized self but to realize a new relationship with the one we already 'have'. In this chapter, he calls this no-self, or as I have rendered it (following Ziporyn), "no-fixed-identity".

What does it mean to have no-fixed-identity? By what means might it be realized? Not surprisingly, Zhuangzi is rather vague on both issues, especially in the case of means. This latter sometimes seems presented as a form of meditation as when Ziqi spaces out and loses his 'me' (2:2) or Yan Hui, after practicing "fasting of the heart-mind", discovers that his 'I' "has not yet begun to exist" (4:12). The anecdotal character of these stories taken together with so many more that make no mention of meditation at all suggests caution in assigning strong advocacy of traditional meditative techniques to Zhuangzi, however. We know from our own times, in any case, that those who do advocate for meditation seem almost incapable of speaking of anything else. What he does more frequently seem to advocate is what I call imaginative envisioning. He asks us to imagine what it would be like to think or feel in a certain way, and that, presumably, might help us to make that perspective our own. Thus, in this chapter he asks us to imagine how it would feel to depend on nothing at all, and this, should we manage to envision it, would assist us toward a growing experiential approximation of that vision in our daily lives. We will have occasion to explore these ideas more thoroughly as they emerge in Zhuangzi's wandering text.

As to the meaning of no-self or no-fixed-identity, this too might best be left to unfold with the text itself. What we can say here, in reference to the portion of text now under consideration, is that Zhuangzi seems more concerned with the descriptive psychological behaviors that exemplify no-fixed-identity than he is in delving into the mechanics of some ostensible concrete transformation. It is principally a cultivated change in perspective, not a sudden experience arriving like a bolt from the blue.

WANDERING FREE IN NON-DEPENDENCE

Zhuangzi now presents us with three examples of those who, because they have a 'normal' sense of self and thus a tentative 'somebody', must continually strive to in fact be that 'somebody'. There is clearly a progressive aspect to these three responses to the need to 'be somebody'. He begins with the most obviously petty egoic project, the pursuit of the esteem of others through the achievement of power, prestige and fame. These are the *external* props that support the egoic-self. Here, I have imported reference to Huizi into the text since Zhuangzi likely had him in mind. The final chapter (the 33rd) of the *Zhuangzi*, a Confucian-leaning syncretistic consideration of the philosophers of the time, finds Huizi alone as not having expressed even a partial participation in the comprehensive "ancient art of the Dao", and this primarily because he is perceived as wholly concerned with achieving a "name". According to this author, Huizi formulated his paradoxes only to wow others. He debated only to defeat others and to thereby gain renown. He sought his identity in things external. Consequentially, he became alienated from his own self: "Hui Shi's talents were fruitlessly dissipated running after things, and never returning to himself" (Ziporyn 2009; p 125). Zhuangzi himself, though he would likely have agreed with much of this criticism, would, I believe, also have completely embraced him as also a full participant in Dao in that his not-oneness was as much One as any other. And, lest we forget, without him there would have been no Zhuangzi as he developed, if we take Zhuangzi's own teaching into account—namely, that their opposition generated each other, and that these two can also be united to form a oneness (2:22).

In our own times we are frequently amazed that those who seem to have reached the pinnacle of success, having achieved fame and wealth, so easily crash and burn in an excess of depression. Might it not be that those who have achieved so much in the realm of the external have consequentially come to realize how ineffective this turns out to be in actually making them a complete and fully real 'somebody'? We who have not reached that pinnacle yet nonetheless still strive in our own petty ways to approximate it may continue to believe that it will achieve this aim. Yet Zhuangzi entreats us to consider the folly of doing so right now wherever we are in the process. It is likely that all of us, should we take the time to engage in a bit of self-inquiry, will discover how we have cultivated an insidious *dependence* on the opinions of others in the construction of our own project of being 'somebody'. Seeing how this is the case, we are able to imagine an alternative.

Zhuangzi's next example presents such an alternative, albeit one that still does not go far enough. The philosopher Song Xing (aka Song Rongzi), a member of the Chia-xia Academy (sponsored by King Xuan (319-310 B.C.E.)) and Zhuangzi's contemporary, might be described as a proto-Daoist in that he advocated for a subjective shift from an emphasis on the 'outer', concerns about the demands of convention and the opinion of others, to the 'inner', the cultivation of one's inherent sense of how best to behave. Perhaps his best known maxim was, "to be insulted is not a disgrace", which I have imported into the text, although Zhuangzi's description of this shift, that he didn't care what the world thought of him, makes the point as well. Broadly speaking, this shift to subjectivity as the best means to human flourishing typified philosophical Daoism's response to the Confucian obsession with conforming to fixed, external norms.

This shift from dependence on things external to the internal, though it may, in our much more individualistic age seem almost axiomatic, can easily enough be put to the test to discover the extent to which it is true in us. How do we respond when insulted? In this way we see how radically challenging and how fundamentally transformative such a freedom would be. Shi Deqing (1546-1623) tells us why: "[Song Xing] was able to forget reputation but had not yet forgotten his fixed identification with his particular self" (Ziporyn 2009; p 131). It is doubtful that Song Xing achieved even this much, given that the fundamental problem still had not been addressed. Zhuangzi is clearly pointing us toward his concluding statement that the sage has no-self.

Zhuangzi offers this as only an exemplary first step toward the complete non-dependence that he envisions. Song Xing still depended on his own self-opinion; he still needed to be 'somebody' in his own estimation. This is a dependence on *performance*; what if we fail of this, as we most certainly will? How could we ever wander free in non-dependence if we depended on success in any activity, even that of wandering free in non-dependence? Though only anecdotally suggested by Zhuangzi, this non-dependence on even non-dependence seems to be the logical next step in non-dependent wandering. Thus I say, we are perfect by virtue of our being perfectly who we are, however imperfect that may be. There are no conditions to meet. In affirming all things as they are, we are non-dependent on their being in any way different than how they are; this includes ourselves.

Zhuangzi says that "even" Song Xing would laugh at the person who lost himself in pursuing the praise of others because he sees in him a valuable step in the direction of non-dependence, but he also sees that it does not go far enough. Wang Fuzhi (1619-1692) identifies this deficiency in yet another way: "Song Rongzi [Xing] did not yet understand how to laugh at himself" (Ziporyn 2009; p131). Such self-directed laughter can demonstrate the freedom of which Zhuangzi speaks. Laughing at ourselves reveals two insights: we fail of our own ideals, and it does not matter. This is non-dependence on non-dependence. Laughter is a natural response of the heart that freely wanders.

We are all like the silly little birds who laugh at the flight of Peng. Can we laugh at that? Can we laugh at ourselves for laughing at others? Laughter can be an expression of self-transcendence; it evinces self-awareness and self-acceptance. Zhuangzi's sage wanders free and unfettered, not because she has 'arrived' at some ideal state, but because she has realized freedom from the futile pursuit of any such thing. Carefree laughter and playfulness are the hallmarks of the Zhuangzian sage. If all is well, why take anything too seriously? If we are perfect in being our imperfect selves, why worry overmuch about those imperfections? Once we can walk this 'road' we can more effectively—and happily—walk the other 'road' of self-cultivation.

Zhuangzi next introduces us to the legendary sage Liezi. This may be the first extant mention of him, and though it seems to refer to a traditional story about his powers, that he "rode the wind", we cannot be sure that Zhuangzi did not make him up, as he did so many others. (Scholars tell us that the book that bears his name was probably compiled in the 4th century C.E.). This need not concern us, however, unless we are enamored of those powers which Zhuangzi goes on to dismiss as irrelevant. Liezi, for all his 'spiritual' powers, still depended on something.

What did he depend on? The wind. But if this is a failing, how can anyone not perpetually and necessarily fail? Peng also depended on the monsoonal winds to take his flight from Oblivion to Oblivion; all life is utterly dependent upon a seemingly infinite number of physical realities outside its own powers. Our dependence in this tenuous world is total. This dependence of Liezi must, therefore, refer to a different level of dependence, a psychological one. He wanted to fly upon the wind, not simply because he could, but because he believed a demonstration of 'spiritual' power was a proof of his sagacity. He still wanted to be a sage. In the end, the pursuit of 'spirituality' is little different than the pursuit of the praise of others or of self-respect. He still wanted to be someone.

Whether a true representation of the man himself or not, Zhuangzi uses Liezi as an archetype of that form of 'spiritual' pursuit that believes overt demonstrations of 'spiritual' power are proof of 'spiritual' realization. Zhuangzi never dismisses these as impossible; indeed he seems to suggest they are actually possible, only he sees them as a distraction. They are but another expression of dependence.

In a lengthy story in the 7th chapter, Zhuangzi makes use of Liezi once again. Here, he becomes so enamored of the prognostic powers of a shaman that he dismisses the way of his own less demonstrative teacher. Only after his teacher makes that shaman flee in fear after exposing him to the depths of his inner emptiness, does Liezi begin to see wherein lays 'true' spirituality. "This time I showed him 'me' before I am 'me'—just an empty, chaotic impulse with no identifiable who or what. That's why he ran away" (7:17). For his part, Liezi had so far failed to understand that true spirituality is no-spirituality, that the so-called 'true self' is no-fixed-self, that the sage is not somebody spiritual, but nobody at all. Zhuangzi summarizes: "Just be empty, nothing more" (7:19).

Having shown us three examples of dependence, each successively more liberated than the one before, he now asks us to imagine a radically different way of being in the world: "But what if you depended on nothing at all? Imagine that. What if you just soared upon whatever seems true of the cosmos and upon everything and anything that happens? How could your soaring ever be brought to a halt" (1:11)?

If this is indeed a statement of Zhuangzi's ultimate vision, is it not curious that he frames it as a hypothetical question? And is it not more curious still that he leaves it unanswered? The further we delve into Zhuangzi, however, the less this will surprise us. He obviously wishes to assist us into an agreement with his take on things, believing that it will occasion a happier and more fruitful life experience for us, but that same 'take' disallows prescribing formulaic answers to life's needs. We must find them in ourselves if they are to be genuine, and they must be genuine if they are to be effective. Thus does he leave things hypothetical, a mere suggestion of a possibility. And thus, too, does the entirety of this work exude a tone of profound ambiguity. This is comparable to the arts of midwifery, the maieutic methods of Socrates and Kierkegaard, where the goal is not the delivery of a 'positive teaching', but rather the creation of an open-ended doubt. And it is, as we might expect, a practical demonstration of the Daoist concept of *wuwei*, non-doing. We must, therefore, scratch our heads and engage with everything he says in an attempt to understand. Who's to say that the conclusions we draw are the ones he had in mind? Does it matter? Perhaps the process itself is more important than the conclusions we draw. In any event, Zhuangzi's ambiguity is clearly purposed as the author of the 33rd chapter observed: "The guidelines within them [his words] are undepletable; giving forth new meanings without shedding the old ones. Vague! Ambiguous! We have not got to the end of them yet" (Ziporyn 2009; p 124).

There is absolutely nothing in the entire universe that is not utterly dependent on a seemingly infinite number of conditions. Given that our dependency in this world is absolute, how can we speak of depending on nothing? It's a question of attitude. We depend on our bodies to keep us alive—but do we depend on living? Can we release our grip on life in such a way as to accept its end with equanimity? To do so is to enjoy a kind of non-dependence. If nothing *has to* happen, then whatever happens is acceptable. This psychological shift to non-dependence opens up a vast field of freedom and enjoyment in which to wander and play.

This is essentially the full extent of Zhuangzi's vision. It's as simple as that. Many interpreters would have him proposing some form of religious project of redemption, of uniting with some Ultimate Dao, or even the attainment of immortality. This, at my reading, is the exact opposite of what Zhuangzi has in mind. Any such project must necessarily depend on a mess of assumptions, none of which could possibly be substantiated either intellectually or experientially. Dependence on the reasoning mind, Zhuangzi suggests in the next chapter, is to depend on the utterly undependable (2:14). Interpreting experience as definitively explaining anything is equivalent to interpreting a dream within a dream (2:56). In the realm of non-dependence, on the other hand, nothing has to be true, nothing needs to be explained. However things actually 'are', whatever seems to 'happen'— these can all be "charioted upon" with equanimity.

But Zhuangzi speaks of charioting on what is "true" of the cosmos, one might protest. Yes, but what is 'true' of the cosmos remains so without any need of our knowing what that is (1:10). We are able to soar upon it not because we know what is true of it (a dependence on knowing), but because we do not know it and need not know it. Perhaps Zhuangzi would have us think back to his question, "Is blue the sky's *true* color" (1:3)? It doesn't matter; when Peng looks down he also sees only blue, but he soars nonetheless. Indeed, rather than being an obstacle to our soaring, our not-knowing becomes the very means by which we do so. It is the fact that we cannot know (or, more accurately, cannot know whether we know or not (2:48)) that facilitates our release into non-dependence—we do not *need* to know. The 'obstacle' of our not-knowing is thus an essential one for Zhuangzi, but his whole point is that any and every obstacle is an occasion for our soaring. Our non-dependence is predicated on our utter, inescapable dependence on all that happens around us and to us.

Finally, it is also worth noting that 'true' (*zheng*) as used here is not intended to convey a factual proposition about reality, but means something more akin to "aligned with" (Ziporyn 2009; p 218-9). Implied is that "true" is a relationship with things, not an idea about them. To chariot upon what is true is to align oneself with events as they arise, and that requires no knowledge of the why or what of them, but only an acceptance of them as they appear to be.

NO-SELF AS NO-FIXED-IDENTITY

We have now arrived at one of the most apparently definitive of Zhuangzi's statements regarding the character of someone who has fully realized his vision. Yet, far from unambiguously clarifying things, this only serves to throw us into an even thornier ambiguity. The sage has no-self; but what does this mean?

Let us begin by reiterating one of our most fundamental points of departure: The Zhuangzian sage is only a hypothetical. Zhuangzi himself was not a sage by his own reckoning. This may disappoint the religious yearning in us for a 'consummate human being', a fully realized guru for us to emulate, but it also frees us from a dependence on any such fantasy (6:10). As only a hypothetical, this definitive representation of the nature of a sage is immediately robbed of its power to fetter us with a dependence on an unrealizable goal. If our wandering depended on the realization of anything, especially some goal of 'enlightenment', then no wandering would ever be possible. The only alternative, therefore, must be that we wander in whatever reality we presently find ourselves. We must wander now, just as we are. If need be, we must wander in our inability to wander. Yet does this not throw us into a nonsensical infinite regress? It does; but when has the actual stuff of living ever made 'sense'?

Why do we wish to wander at all? We desire to more fully enjoy our lives, an affirmable goal in that it is the process of life itself. Self-inquiry, however, will also most certainly uncover in this aspiration a desire to be 'somebody'—the desire to be *seen to be* a 'sage'. But the sage is a nobody. It is here, therefore, that the work must be done, and this is why Zhuangzi sums it all up by telling us the sage has no-self.

We have yet to consider what this entails. Let us begin by saying that no-self does not mean no self. Ziqi declares, "*I* have lost me" (2:2). When Yan Hui practices "fasting of the heart-mind", *he* declares "*I* have not yet begun to exist" (4:12). In both cases there remains a self in relationship to itself; only that relationship has changed. Instead of taking their selves as fixed and static identities, they have come to see them as "temporary lodgings" (2:61). This is the realization of "no-fixed-identity". Identity there is, but it is appreciated as only a passing phenomenon that need not be grasped as something that can be lost. We see this in a metaphorical description of a sage-king: "Sometimes he thinks he's a horse, other times he thinks he's an ox—he has no-fixed-identity and thus sees no need to impose himself upon others" (7:2). And we see it in those on their deathbeds who contentedly release themselves into the next transformation (6:14ff). Identified with the cosmos as ceaseless transformation, their own transformation incurs no loss.

No-self is thus equivalent to no-fixed-identity, and this is participating in the experience of being a self without clinging to it as anything other than a passing phenomenon. It is a relationship that allows for our carefree and playful wandering in the identity that we presently find ourselves to 'be'. It is a psychological movement, not a metaphysical one.

Wang Fuzhi (1619-1692) succinctly sums up the more obvious implications of non-dependence and its correspondence to no-fixed-identity: "[T]his is what it means to be free of dependence: not leaning on things to establish some identity for oneself, not leaning on projects to establish some merit for oneself, not leaning on actualities to establish some name for oneself" (Ziporyn 2009; p129).

REFLECTIONS—PART THREE

FOUR ILLUSTRATIVE STORIES

The chapter concludes with four stories illustrating the themes already discussed and introduces another, Zhuangzi's signature "usefulness of the useful". The first addresses the folly of the pursuit of 'name' (a fixed-identity) through political power. The final three more closely reflect the themes of the Peng myth, especially the trope of the small consciousness scoffing at the large consciousness, the autobiographical character of which is seen in the last two stories in which Zhuangzi's friend Huizi is the scoffer.

The first story is pregnant with all manner of Daoist themes. Yao, a patron saint of the Confucians, was praised for his having ceded his empire to Shun on the basis of his merit, rather than to his own son. Zhuangzi mocks this by suggesting that Shun was only Yao's second best choice and came only after a sage of Daoist stripe refused it. Why did he refuse the empire? Because the empire had no need of an exercise of overt power since the sage's unseen charismatic influence had already occasioned its flourishing. This is a common Daoist theme and represents the power of *wuwei*, non-coercive doing, in the political world. Did Zhuangzi actually believe in such powers? I'd like to think not, but we cannot know. We do know, from the 4th chapter, however, that he did believe in the effectiveness "non-being the change" on a more personal level.

If the empire had no need of the sage's overt exercise of power, then the only reason he would have accepted the reins of power would be for the "name", the prestige and respect it would bring him. But if he depended on that, he'd be nothing more than a guest, wholly dependent on the whims of fortune. Today's hero is tomorrow's villain. The metaphors of the bird content with a branch and the mole with a belly-full of water illustrate the contentedness of those who do not depend on the accumulation of things external. Only those who know what is enough can know contentment. And only those who do not depend on even that can wander free.

In the second story, the madman Jieyu relates to Jian Wu a fantastic story of a sage who only subsists on wind and dew. Wu, who thinks the story a lot of ridiculous "big talk", in his turn, relates it to Lian Shu who chastens him for his blindness in spiritual matters.

But the story *is* so fantastic as to be ridiculous. In addition to subsisting on only wind and dew, this sage hitches his chariot to dragons so as to wander beyond the known world. The parallels here with Peng and the sage's charioting upon all dependence so as to wander are immediately clear. But what are we to do with the fact that it is absurdly fantastic? Wu has declared himself unable to believe it, yet Shu, presumably himself a sage, gladly endorses it.

Zhuangzi is having fun at our expense. If we believe that it matters whether these stories must either be believable or unbelievable, true or false, then we are still depending on our reason in an attempt to make 'sense' of the world. In the end, Zhuangzi doesn't believe that any of it is 'true'. No such sage exists. It is not true that Jieyu spoke to Wu. Neither Jieyu nor Wu as represented ever existed (though Jieyu appears in the *Analects* (18:5) where he makes fun of Confucius). Through fantastic stories, Zhuangzi hopes to bring us face to face with our own not-knowing. Our integration with our being in a world, our harmony in the life experience, cannot be realized through formulaic propositions of 'truth'. This can only happen organically, through release into the life process itself.

Wu's rejection of Jieyu's "big talk" parallels the tiny birds scoffing at Peng's incredible flight and Huizi's similar rejection of Zhuangzi's "big talk" as illustrated in concluding two stories. Though often seemingly irreconcilably divergent, there are frequently subtle threads of relevance that knit these stories together.

The story also makes yet another reference to the politically beneficial effects of *wuwei*. Wang Fuzhi is able to show this political spin as a further elucidation of the idea of no-fixed-identity: "[T]hose who see themselves internally as having one fixed identity believe there is a world existing outside themselves, and those for whom there is a 'world' on the one hand relating to 'oneself' on the other will use that self to try to rule the world" (Ziporyn 2009; p 134). Trying to rule the world need not be trying to become an emperor, but simply attempting to impose oneself on things and others. "But", Wang warns, "one who does not allow others to wander far and unfettered can never do so himself" (Ziporyn 2009; p 135).

In the next two stories we have Huizi demonstrating his bondage to reason and, consequentially, to conventional ideas of usefulness. Zhuangzi's "big words" are useless. Why? Because they do not deal with 'reality' and cannot further the advance of human ambition. But Zhuangzi, with an altogether different perspective on what makes for a happy life, offers two advantages that demonstrate the usefulness of the useless. The more mundane of these is simply that usefulness leads to being used and abused. Huizi's "stink tree" survives because it is useless. And there is much to be said for survival (though we needn't depend on it!). More important to Zhuangzi's vision, however, is that uselessness reflects a release from dependence on any and all worldly outcomes. Carefree wandering precludes believing that one must be useful to have a 'worthwhile' life. If this does not seem like an inexcusable slap in the face to a central human value, then I have failed to express it well. Yet, when the dust settles, Zhuangzi would argue that, *wuwei*, non-being the change, is much more effective than trying to be it. Usefulness is used. Usefulness uses. What uses, also abuses. What is abused, abuses in return. What is pushed pushes back.

Perhaps the best place to begin to understand what is implied by the usefulness of the useless is to look at the largest context conceivable. The classic metaphors are found in the *Laozi*: "Thirty spokes make a wheel, yet it is the emptiness at their hub that makes it useful. . . . Doors and windows are empty space, but they alone make a room useful. Thus, something is made useful by virtue of the useless." "The Dao is empty; we use it but it is never emptied" (XI, IV; my adaptations). Metaphysical Dao, the unnamable and unimaginable Mystery, is the supremely Useless—yet it is only in taking account of It that things have any context at all. This was perhaps the most profound insight of philosophical Daoism. Previously, it was believed that in *knowing* 'Heaven' we could make use of it. The proto-Daoists realized that it is in our *not-knowing* it that it becomes useful. As beings with emptiness at our core we can either attempt to orient ourselves to a Ground of Being, something known, or to Emptiness, something unknowable. Daoism chooses Emptiness—I will leave the reader to decide which more closely follows our actual existential experience. The essence of the Daoist experience, therefore, is release into the Unknowable, and this, for Zhuangzi, equates to thankfully and playfully following along with whatever unfolds in non-dependence on any particular outcome.

Another way to imagine this is through the concepts of Yin and Yang where Yang is being/usefulness and Yin is non-being/uselessness. Daoism prioritizes orientation toward Yin. Why? Because human *beings* are all about yang-ing—doing and knowing—and have sought to compensate for their inner yin, the emptiness at their core, by simply engaging in more yang-ing. This amounts to the relentless pursuit of being a concrete 'someone' when no such outcome is possible. Philosophical Daoism acknowledges the futility of such a project and instead harmonizes with the human experience as it actually manifests—just another temporary expression of the ever-transforming.

This is the foundational meaning of the usefulness of the useless which informs every aspect of the philosophical Daoist's orientation to herself and to the world. Embedded in Mystery, what is not mystery? In as much as the human experience is unresolvedly tenuous—utterly ungrounded—why not harmonize with that experience and thereby cast off the burden of the relentless pursuit of something fixed and sure?

CHAPTER TWO
REALIZING THE VIEW FROM DAO

THE TEXT—PART ONE

SEEING THE EQUALITY OF THINGS AND IDEAS

1 Yancheng Ziyou found his master, Ziqi of the Southern Wall, reclining against a low table all spaced out as if he had lost part of himself. "Something has clearly changed with you!" exclaimed Yan. "Is it really possible for one's body to become like dead wood, and one's mind like dead ashes?"

2 Ziqi replied, "That's a great question, Yan! What happened is that I just lost 'me'! Do you understand? If you only hear the piping of man, and not the piping of the earth, not to mention the piping of Heaven, how could you?"

3 "Please explain further," replied Ziyou.

4 "When the Great Clod belches forth the life force it is like the wind in the forest. As soon as the wind arises all the empty hollows in the trees begin to make their piping, each one making its own unique sound according to its sculpture. Together they make a great harmony, softly in a light breeze, loudly in a tempest. And when the wind has passed, they all return to their empty silence. Surely, you've seen how the voices of all these trees contend with one another?"

5 "So, the sounds made by the trees must be the 'piping of the earth' and the 'piping of man' must be that made by instruments; but what is the 'piping of Heaven?'" asked Ziyou.

6 "Ah! That's crux of the matter!" answered Ziqi. "It seems that among the myriad things each one chooses its own piping and we cannot discover a Who or What behind it. But if this is true of the world, it must also be true of 'me'. Realizing this, I lost my 'me'—there is no fixed and identifiable 'me'!"

THE TEXT—PART TWO

7 An open-awareness decoupled from a fixed-identity has no need for accomplishments and embraces all things. A closed-awareness bound to a fixed-self is narrow and insular. 'Big words' like mine seem bland and useless. Small words have much to say, but break the world into pieces—and ourselves with it.

8 Human beings tend to dwell in the latter. Asleep, we are at peace; awake, the ceaseless struggle continues—one struggle following on the heels of another. We are filled with fear. Small fears gnaw at our minds; big fears leave us is despair. We are quick to judge right and wrong, clinging to these judgments as if they were eternal truths, hoping this will also make *us* 'real'. We daily seem to wear away and compensate with yet more activities. As if fettered, we follow the same ruts, unable to change. Our minds are left half-dead, and we can find no remedy.

9 All this human activity, all these emotions—joy and anger, sadness and happiness, hopes and regrets—, every spontaneous joy or calculated pretension, all these are just like the piping issuing from the empty hollows in the forest. And like their piping, we have no idea from whence our own arises. Is this then all there is to existence? It's true that without the unknowable there would be no 'me', but it is also true that without 'me' there would be no expression of the unknowable to ask about it. This seems to be an obvious 'proof' of some 'Controller', but whatever it is remains unknowable. If it has a reality, then it is only emptily so.

10 The same applies when we consider our own bodies. Of the many organs, does one rule over all the rest? Or do they take turns ruling? We

cannot find the controller. Does it matter? Whatever is the case, despite our not-knowing, the body lives on just the same. Can we not similarly just allow our conscious selves to trustingly let the process unfold?

11 If, on the other hand, we take our self to be a fixed and static reality, complete in itself, then we will spend our lives continually worrying about the day it will end. Everything around us becomes a threat, grinding on us, injuring us. Yet it all goes by like a galloping horse. Life is so sad! So we labor ceaselessly trying to be a fixed somebody, but in the end no success is possible. When someone dies people say, "He still lives in our hearts." But in truth his body decayed and his mind went with it. This is our greatest sorrow. Isn't human experience completely bewildering? Or is it only I that find it so? No, my guess is that every human being finds both life and death bewildering.

12 If we take our own mind as our teacher and see the theories it adopts as complete and sufficient to make sense of life, well then who could be said to have no teacher? But the mind just picks out a tiny bit of the endless process of change and can never see the whole. The fool also makes his selection—so he too can be said to have his teacher!

13 If we think that right and wrong exist before our minds deem them so, that's like believing Huizi's paradox: I left for Yue today and arrived there yesterday. This is equivalent to calling the non-existent existent, something even beyond the understanding of the sage Emperor Yu—how could I begin to understand it?

14 Hold on, you might say: human speech is not just a lot of hot air; what we say and explain about the world has some truth and meaning to it. Yes, this is true; but it is also the case that everything is strangely unfixed; like the things we describe, our understanding is also always in flux. For that matter, do words ever reach the things they describe? So, have we really described something, or not? You believe that human speech is different than the chirping of baby birds, but is there a sense in which they are in fact the same? When we understand how they are the same, we wonder if our differences of opinion are really ultimately different at all.

15 How could it be that our understanding of the various daos could be so darkened that we consider some genuine and others erroneous? How could our understanding of the various theories be so darkened that we deem some right and others wrong? (Would you say the same for the piping of the forest's trees?) Where can we go without that being a dao? What can we say without that in some sense being affirmable? The problem arises when we take our daos and words as final and complete—as the 'right way' and the 'truth'. Our theories are darkened by our linking them to our need to 'be somebody' right.

16 Thus, we have the competing rights and wrongs of the Confucians and Mohists who affirm what the other negates and negate what the other affirms. But if we want to affirm what they both negate (that both can be right) and negate what they both affirm (that one must be right and the other wrong) then nothing works so well as shining the light of the obvious upon them. (Just appreciate how their chirpings are like those of the baby birds or the sounds of the trees stirred by the wind—all equally affirmable.)

17 We think of our theory as 'this', as right, and the other's theory as 'that', as wrong. But everyone and everything is clearly both a 'this' and a 'that', so in this sense they are the same. But we cannot easily see another's 'that' as a 'this' being bound as we are by our own subjectivity, by our own 'this'. Still, we can see how a 'this' generates a 'that' and a 'that' generates a 'this'. Each requires and gives rise to the other. We can call this the simultaneous generation of opposites. But just as they generate each other, so also do they destroy each other in as much as every 'this' is also a 'that'. Similarly, our affirming of one thing is the negation of something else, yet because this is reversible, both are affirmable and both can be negated. So also do right and wrong create and destroy each other.

18 For this reason, the sage does not participate in all this 'this-ing' and 'that-ing' but rather lets all things be illuminated by the light of a higher view, the obvious equality of things. In this way, she can affirm everything and just let them be their own 'this'. (All things taken together is 'THIS', so every individual thing is also 'this'.)

34

19 Confused? Let me try and say it in a different way. 'Every 'this' is also someone else's 'that' and every 'that' is also someone else's 'this'. Each 'this' has its own right and wrong and each 'that' has its own right and wrong. We must ask, therefore, if there is really any true distinction between 'this' and 'that' or between their respective rights and wrongs. When we are able to see that sense in which they are no longer opposites, this can be called Dao as Convergence, the point of view that allows all daos to converge into a oneness. This point of view is like being at the center of a circle from which one can respond with equanimity to the endless parade of rights and wrongs that spin around one. This is why I said that shining the light of the obvious equality of things on our understanding of the world can be so helpful.

20 Now logicians like Huizi and Gongsun Long make much of the inability of words to accurately parse and represent reality. The latter tells us that a pointing finger cannot point out itself (can't free itself from its own subjectivity) and that "a white horse is not a horse" ('white' and 'horse' being distinct categories). I say: Using *this* finger to show that a finger is not a finger is not as good as using *not-this* finger (that is, *that* finger) to show how a finger is not a finger. Similarly, using *this* horse to show that a horse is not a horse is not as good as using *not-this* horse (that is, *that* horse) to show how a horse is not a horse. When 'this' and 'that' cancel out each other, Heaven and earth are one finger. All things are one horse.

THE TEXT—PART THREE

21 Something is 'right' only because someone deems it so. Something is 'wrong' only because someone says it is. Daos (ways) come to be when people walk them. Things are 'the way they are' because we understand them as such. They are so because people say they are so. Every individual thing can in some sense be said to be 'so', and that 'so' can in some sense be affirmed as good and acceptable.

22 Thus, every individual thing can be said to be 'right' and 'acceptable'. If we say that this thing is a 'beam' and not a 'pillar', or that a leper is ugly and the famous beauty Xishi is beautiful, there is still a perspective from which someone can say that the opposite is true. Thus, there is yet another dao that allows these two perspectives (daos) to open up into each other, and to thereby combine to form a oneness.

23 Separating out some things unites other things. Uniting some things separates other things. Creating one thing destroys something else. Destroying one thing creates something else. Thus, in some sense nothing is either created or destroyed, but rather these can be united to form a oneness.

24 Only someone who experiences this uniting into oneness can 'understand' it. Such a person does not impose her definition of 'rightness' on the world and its 'things' but rather affirms them all just as they are and allows them to be just as they are. Seen from the point of view of Dao, their ordinary reality is understood as united with every other ordinary reality and this enables the affirmation of all things. This view from Dao is also just a point of view, and not an imposition of a definition of 'rightness' or 'correctness' upon the world. Viewing things thusly, as a matter of course, and not because you consider it the 'right dao', is Dao.

25 Striving to *make* things 'one' (through mental exercises, like my friend Huizi does and as I appear to do here! or through various 'spiritual' exercises like so many of our contemporaries) without realizing how all views, whatever they may be, are also united in a oneness can be seen in the parable I call "Three in the Morning".

26 A monkey trainer told his monkeys that he would give them three nuts in the morning and four nuts in the evening. The monkeys were outraged! Okay, the monkey trainer said, I'll give you *four* in the morning and three in the evening. The monkeys were overjoyed! The monkey trainer realized that whichever arrangement was affirmed nothing was lost. Yet, since the monkeys were sure that one was better than the other, he just allowed their 'this' to be 'This'. In this way the sage harmonizes with the

various rights and wrongs of others while herself remaining in the center of the heavenly potter's wheel, where all rights and wrongs are equalized so that all things can be affirmed.

27 I call this Walking Two Roads.

THE TEXT—PART FOUR

28 Philosophers like to make much of a 'golden past' in proof of their points, so here's my version:

29 The ancients managed to arrive at the ultimate understanding. What was it? They believed that nothing exists. Period. This is perfect—nothing more can be added, nothing more can be said.

30 But then simplicity started to devolve into complexity, as they tend to do with humans. Next, came those who said that things exist, but that they were all One and could not be divided one from the other; there are no boundaries between them.

31 Next came along those who said that there were boundaries between things, but that no right and wrong could be assigned to them.

32 Finally, we arrived at the view that things exist, have definite and discrete boundaries, and that some are right and others wrong. When rights and wrongs waxed bright and completely defined how we see the world, the view from Dao waned and grew dim. This loss of the view from Dao is precisely what caused the ceaseless disquiet seen in our need to cling to some things while rejecting others and in our constant worry about benefit and harm, gain and loss.

33 But is there really any waning as opposed to waxing? Or is there a sense in which they, too, can be united to form a oneness? On one level there is waxing and waning; yet on another level there is no waxing and waning. Take, for example, Zhao Wen's zither playing, Kuangzi's rhythm keeping, and Huizi's desk-slumping; all three excelled in their

arts and found their sense of self in them—attempted to be 'somebody' through them. This was their waxing. But others did not, of course, share their enthusiasm for the supreme value of these successes, so they needed to convince them in order to validate their sense of self-worth. Thus Huizi, among others, ended up endlessly debating about such obscure ideas as 'hardness and whiteness', and Zhao Wen's son, despite his father's insistence, proved unable to master his father's zither. This was their waning.

34 So, can we say they actually accomplished something that finally made their lives full and complete? If so, I and everyone else can be considered a complete success. Or, are we to think of their lives as utter failures? If so, then I and everyone else are likewise complete failures. However, might there be a sense in which there is neither success nor failure, but only things being what they are, and in that, being utterly successful?

35 Thus does the sage aim for the realization of a profound radiance in the equalizing submergence of all human aspiration. She does not make fixed judgments about things, but just lets them be what they are. This again is shining the light of the obvious to show the equality of things.

36 Now I will attempt some words to explain what I mean when I speak of seeing the entire world as an affirmable "This". However, when I call everything This, there automatically appears to be something not included, a 'that'. So, let's include that in our This—yet this forms but another category which begs yet another. And, in any case, our This is really no different than That. This is the way of words.

37 Even though this inadequacy of words is unavoidable, I ask your indulgence to try a say something about This. Let's say there is a beginning for the world. If this is the case, then there is also a not-yet-beginning-to-be-a beginning. In which case there is also a not-yet-beginning-to-   be-a-not-yet-beginning-to-be-a-beginning. Similarly, if we say there is existence, there is also nonexistence. Then there is also a not-yet-beginning-to-be-nonexistence. And then there is a not-yet-beginning-to-not-yet-beginning-to-be-nonexistence.   Anyway,

suddenly, nonexistence exists! I'm now lost and don't know whether existence is nonexistence or the other way around!

38 So, now I have said what I wanted to say. But I do-not-yet-know whether I have actually said something meaningful or whether I have said nothing meaningful at all. Words are useful, but they always miss the mark.

39 So, let's exclaim with Huizi and friends: "There is nothing larger than the tip of an autumn hair, and Mt. Tai is tiny!" "No one lives longer than a dead child, and Pengzu died young!" "Heaven, earth and I were born at the same moment, and I and everything else make One!" All 'true'—from a certain point of view!

40 Ah, but if these are 'true', can words really say anything about them? Doesn't *saying* that One exists negate this One? Yet I have spoken, so the One and my words make two, and now I make them three, and on it goes until even a master mathematician would soon lose count, how much more a common man like me! And if moving from the nonexistence of One to its existence we so quickly arrive at three, how much higher will be the count if we move from one existence to another! So, let's not verbally move from anywhere to anywhere, but rather let's just affirmingly accept all we encounter as This. Let's just say Yes!

41 The view from Dao has no borders within or without. Words have no sure and constant meaning. Yet, we use them to create boundaries. All our rights and wrongs, all our endless debates about reality, these are the stuff of words, and we consider their use our greatest human virtue. Now the sage, she figures that 'something' exists beyond all knowing, but she sees no point in debating about it or believing anything in particular about it. As for what exists within the range of knowability, she's happy to discuss it, but does not cling to any one opinion about it. As for the doings of humanity, she has an opinion, but does not fight for it.

42 When something is carved off, something is left uncarved. When debate settles something, something else is left out. What's left out is always the most important thing of all. What is it? The sage hides it in her

embrace and does not divide it with words. Most people feel obliged to try and prove it to others, but this just leaves it left out once again.

43 Great Dao cannot be spoken. Great debate is wordless. Great humaneness is not humane. Great morality is not picky. Great courage is not violent. For when Dao is explained it ceases to be Dao. When debate uses words it brings no closure. When humaneness is imposed it fails as such. When morality is picky it excludes others. When courage is violent it solves nothing. These five begin as affirmably round, but inevitably end up square and full of sharp corners.

44 Therefore, when the rationalizing mind restfully settles in what it cannot know, it has fully realized itself. The proof that uses no words, the Dao that is not-a-dao—who can 'know' them? The ability to in some sense 'understand' these I call tapping the Heavenly Reservoir. It is poured into, but never full, partaken of, but never emptied. Yet we are ever-not-knowing from whence it comes. It is simply life itself.

45 Let's call it The Dark Brilliance.

THE TEXT—PART FIVE

46 Here are some stories that help illustrate what I mean:

47 Long ago Yao asked the advice of Shun concerning his obsessive desire to conquer a few nearby minor kingdoms. "Why not just allow them to continue out there in the wilderness?" suggested Shun. "Long ago ten suns rose in the sky and all things everywhere were brightly illuminated. How much better are multitudes of expressions of Dao than many suns!"

48 Toothless asked Wang Ni, "Do you know that upon which all things agree?" Wang Ni replied, "How could I possibly know that!?" "Well then," continued Toothless, "Do you know that you do not know anything?" "How could I possibly know that!?" answered Wang Ni. "Is

then no knowledge possible at all?" asked Toothless. "How could I possibly know that!?" he replied.

49 "Just the same, let me use some words to try and approximate some understanding of this," continued Wang Ni. "How can I know whether or not what I think is knowing is not really not-knowing? How can I know whether or not what I think is not-knowing is not really knowing? Still, let me share something of what I think I know. When human beings sleep in the cold and damp they wake up in pain—but is this also true of eels? When human beings climb trees, they tremble with fear—but is this also true of monkeys? Which of these three knows the best place to be? People eat their livestock, deer forage for sprouts, snakes eat insects, raptors like mice. Of these four, which one knows what is best to eat? Male monkeys like female monkeys, bucks mate with does, male fish play with female fish, and humans think certain women are great beauties—yet when fish see them they take to the depths, when birds see them they take to the skies, and when deer see them they take to the woods. Which of these four knows what it truly beautiful? From my perspective, all definitions of humaneness and correctness, and of right and wrong, are all hopelessly tangled and confused. How could I figure out which is the 'best' one among them?"

50 "Well, if that is the case," exclaimed Toothless, "then you can't even know what's beneficial for you or what is harmful! Does a fully aware person then make no distinction between benefit and harm!?"

51 "The fully aware person is ultimately free of such concerns," replied Wang Ni. "Lakes might burst into flames, but she cares not about being burned. Rivers may freeze, but she cares not about being cold. Thunder might split mountains and winds raise monstrous seas, but she is not bothered. She chariots on the wind and clouds, rides the sun and moon, and wanders beyond the knowable world. Even life and death are equal for her, how could she then entertain the petty worries of benefit and harm!?"

52 Nervous Magpie spoke to High Tree about Confucius's criticism of the 'Daoist' vision: "The Master criticized the belief that the sage does

not seek accomplishments, cares nothing for benefit or harm, does not seek happiness, and does not follow any one dao. That her not-saying is saying and that her saying is not-saying; and that thus does she wander beyond the dust and dirt. Confucius thought this vision ridiculous, but I think it describes the realization of the Mysterious Dao. What do you think of these words?"

53 "I think your agreement with them negates them!" answered High Tree. "Even the Yellow Emperor could not fathom them; how much less so could Confucius. And you, since you so quickly 'agree' with them, clearly have counted your chickens before they have hatched. How could goalless-ness be furthered by making 'realization of the Mysterious Dao' your goal?"

54 "Still, I will be reckless and speak of this, but you must similarly listen recklessly," continued High Tree. "The sage stands together with the sun and moon, puts time and space beneath her arms, lets the messiness of the world find its own chosen fit, and honors the lowest peasant as equal to everyone else. While the multitudes slave away trying to 'make things better', though she seems like a lazy bum, it is she who participates in and enjoys all things as they are in allowing them to be a single affirmable Lump. In this way she enfolds all things within herself."

55 "As for caring nothing about benefit and harm, how do we even know that our obsessive clinging to life is not delusional? How do we know that hating death is not like being an orphaned exile who has forgotten his way home? When Lady Yi was first captured and brought to Qin she wept copiously, but after some time sharing the king's bed and eating fine foods she wondered that she had wept at all. How do we know that the dead don't similarly regret having clung to life?"

56 "It is said, 'If you dream of making merry, in the morning you will weep. If you dream of weeping, in the morning you will have fun hunting.' While dreaming you don't know it's a dream, and you might even interpret your dream within the dream. But when you wake up, you realize it was all a dream. Perhaps we will all have a great awakening and discover that it's all been a dreaming. Yet, the foolishly wise believe they

are already fully awake and thus take social position as fixed and real. You and Confucius are both dreaming! And I am dreaming too! So, when you say you 'agree' with these words it's as if you were writing their epitaph. Maybe a great sage will one day appear and explain all these mysteries, yet isn't it enough that they are already revealed in every dawn and dusk?"

57 "But suppose you and I decide to debate these things. If I win and you lose or you win and I lose, does that settle the matter? Does one of us have to be right and the other wrong? Couldn't we both be right, or both be wrong? Since neither you nor I can know the answers, how could a third party be of any help? How could their agreement with you or I or disagreement with us both settle the matter? None of us can know; should we then wait for some august Sage to explain it all for us? Or should we rather simply play and wander in the mystery of it all?"

58 "Let's return now to Ziqi's forest. All the trees' voices are utterly dependent on what cannot be known; so isn't this the same as being non-dependent? The theories of the debaters are also completely dependent on each other—one's 'this' generating the other's 'that', and vice versa. Yet, doesn't this universal mutual dependence also render them non-dependent? We can, therefore, harmonize with all these natural expressions. But this means allowing that 'right' is also 'not-right', for if 'right' were truly right, there would be no counter-poised 'not-right', and no need for debate at all. So, harmonize with them all in their natural expressions, follow along with their limitless manifestations. This will bring you the peace that allows you to fully live out your allotted years."

59 "But no! Forget the counting of years; forget 'rightness'! Roam in the give-and-take of boundlessness, for we are all securely lodged together in that boundlessness."

60 Penumbra said to Shadow, "First you walk, then you stand, then you sit, and then you stand again! Why can't you yourself decide on one thing to do?" Shadow replied, "Am I depending on something else to be who I am? And does that something I depend on depend on something else? Is this apparent dependence like a snake's dependence on its shed skin, or a

cicada's dependence on its cast off shell? How could I know why I do as I do?"

61 Zhuang Zhou (that's 'me'—I think!) dreamt he was a butterfly. This butterfly fluttered about just like any butterfly would, totally oblivious to the existence of Zhuang Zhou. Suddenly Zhuang Zhou awoke as himself in the flesh, but greatly bewildered. Was he Zhou who had just dreamt he was a butterfly, or was he a butterfly now dreaming he was Zhou!? Clearly, these are two distinct identities. This is what can be called transformation—one's present identity being only a temporary lodging.

REFLECTIONS—PART ONE

MYSTICISM WITHOUT METAPHYSICS

This second chapter is a favorite among scholars and philosophers, it being largely a discussion of the limitations of reason, logic and language. In it, Zhuangzi reveals his deep skepticism regarding the ability of the rational mind to adequately make sense of the human experience, and thus to provide us with a sustainable *raison d'etre*. Much debate centers on the depth and species of this skepticism. As important as these debates may be, however, they frequently miss the point of Zhuangzi's having opened the discussion in the first place. That point is found in the chapter's title and in the opening story of Ziqi losing his 'me' and his explanation of that experience through the metaphor of the voices, the *debates*, of the forest's trees. But these, like the myth of Peng's fantastic flight, have a clearly mystical dimension, and mysticism is a fearful thing for the rationalizing mind.

There is a definite direction in which Zhuangzi is continually nudging us, and that might best be described as an essentially mystical re-integration with life and its context. Zhuangzi is a mystic; he advocates for an inner movement away from the fetters of the dichotomizing mind and into a sense of joyful, carefree oneness. This mysticism, however, should not be confused with traditional forms of mysticism that promise a resolution to our existential burdens through union with an imagined Ultimate. Zhuangzi's mysticism is utterly innocent of all metaphysics. Indeed, it is through the absence of any and all pretense of such a possibility of escaping our own essential mystery that his mysticism finds the wind upon which to soar. Thus, in advocating for a sense of oneness, he never presumes to posit a One. That would be to *depend* upon something—something believed in, or something believed to be known. Zhuangzi's sense of oneness, like his Dao, is a psychological, perspectival experience. It is not 'the answer'. It makes no claim to describing things as they actually 'are'.

Like much in Zhuangzi, the meaning of this title, "Seeing the Equality of Things and Ideas", is ambiguous and can be parsed in a variety of ways. Though it is intended to summarize the topic of the chapter, we must, therefore, use the chapter to clarify it, and the rendering offered here seems to me to accomplish its intended purpose. "Seen from the point of view of their sameness, all things are one" (5:4), Zhuangzi later tells us. This simple exercise is the central method and intended outcome of this chapter. The experience of realizing that sense in which all things and all our opinions about them are equal is liberating. However, at the same time, it is in no way the negation of the very real differences between things and opinions. Zhuangzi calls the ability to simultaneously appreciate both the equality of things and their diversity Walking Two Roads, a conceptual thread that runs throughout his philosophy and informs and re-grounds all its apparently other-worldly pronouncements. The view from Dao, as I call this 'higher' perspective of the equality of things, enables the fullest engagement in the messiness of the world without being overcome and submerged by it. When we understand that sense in which nothing matters (for nothing is lost however things arrange themselves), we can engage with the world as if everything matters (because in and for the world, everything does matter) without the loss of our inner peace.

A WALK IN THE WOODS AND THE LOSS
OF ONE'S 'ME'

The chapter begins with a disciple finding his master, Ziqi, so spaced out that he wonders if he has realized what might be a formulaic description of an intended meditative outcome: "A body like dead wood and a mind like dead ashes." But Ziqi simply replies that he has lost his 'me'. He goes on to explain this experience by way of a metaphor involving the sounds of the trees in response to the unseen wind. Since this does not immediately seem to address how Ziqi lost his 'me' we are required to imagine how it might be made to do so. I have consequently imported the final interpretive sentence. Having established that the trees seem to have chosen their own unique responses without any identifiable Agent guiding them, he concludes, "Realizing this, I lost my 'me'—there is no fixed and identifiable 'me'!" Behind all his doing, Ziqi can find no fixed and sure doer. All things seem to spontaneously arise, and no ultimate cause can be found for any of them. When the wind stops, the tree's themselves return to their "emptiness". As it is with the cosmos, so too is it with the forest and with Ziqi. Ziqi is a happening; his 'me' is revealed as only the imagined agent of this happening and consequently falls away.

Zhuangzi would have us take an imaginative walk in the woods and simply do what comes to us naturally, namely appreciate it and all its parts just as they are—equal and affirmable simply because they 'are'. A forest is, from a certain point of view, an incredible mess. There are living trees, and dead trees; standing trees and fallen trees; healthy trees and diseased trees; some seem well-formed, while others are twisted, broken or lightening-struck. Yet all these trees, however they appear, are the forest; without them there would be no forest. We affirm them all when we affirm the forest. Zhuangzi understands the cosmos as we do this forest; it and everything that has happened within it is now necessary because it has happened, and because they have happened, they are all equal and affirmable. The cosmos is this forest; its every manifestation is affirmable. Humanity is this forest; we are invited to view our collective arising just as we would the 'mess' of the forest. We are each one of us the forest; we are invited to affirm ourselves just as we are. This is the view from Dao, that perspective which says 'yes' to everything that emerges, however they emerge, because they so emerge. All is well in the Great Mess.

We find this perspective relatively natural and simple when we consider Nature, but not so easy when we attempt to similarly bring it to bear on humanity and ourselves. Observing an anthill, we are able to enjoy the antics of ants without judging some as right and others as wrong; we affirm ants as they are because they are so. Zhuangzi invites us to do the same with humanity. Yet, we insist that the uniquely human obsession with right and wrong is somehow written in the heavens. This, Zhuangzi tells us, is nonsensical: "If we think that right and wrong exist before our minds deem them so, that's like believing Huizi's paradox: "I left for Yue today and arrived there yesterday" (2:13). Nevertheless, we find this movement incredibly difficult to make. If nothing else, this difficulty offers us an opportunity to explore the depth of our sense of exceptionalism and our obsession—Zhuangzi would say fettered obsession—with right and wrong. Curiously, this addiction to right and wrong appears as the most difficult for us to break, more so than even our addiction to the rationalizing mind. For this very reason he frequently lays it before us, challenging us to imagine a point of view where right and wrong do not rule us. For they do. Yuan Hongdao (1568-1610) vividly expresses how this is so: "Between heaven and earth there is nothing free of rights and wrongs. The world is a city of rights and wrongs. The body and mind are a house of rights and wrongs. Wisdom, stupidity, worthiness, worthlessness are the fruits of rights and wrongs. All history is a deserted battlefield of rights and wrongs. The people of the world drown and float in rights and wrongs, wrongs and rights, clinging to their rotting remnants, dangling like fat insects from the ends of branches" (Ziporyn 2009; pp135-6). We fear that realizing an amoral perspective on the world of humanity (one already easily exercised in the case of Nature) will render us immoral; but this fear only further illustrates the depth of our addiction. Zhuangzi would also remind us, however, that to understand right and wrong as purely human inventions does not require us to abandon them, any more than we need abandon reason because of its limits. We are rather invited to end our dependence upon them so as to realize a new relationship with them. As human beings we must of necessity make use of such moral discriminations, but when we understand them in the context of their relativity our peace is not so easily disturbed by them. Again, we are invited to walk two roads.

An appreciative walk in the woods is a mystical experience. It needn't be earth-shattering to be so; the simple experience of thankfully affirming it just as it is, is to momentarily transcend our everyday inclination to divide and judge things and events according to our preferences. What if we were to now see ourselves as also part of that forest? Would we not also be affirmed just as we are? I will not argue for this also being a mystical experience; one who deeply imagines it can describe it as he or she wishes—the point is to experience it. We might describe this as something 'gained', but it also entails a 'loss'. In identifying with the forest in this way something of the insular experience of 'me' dissolves. In what follows, Zhuangzi will repeatedly suggest we learn to see how opposites can be united "to form a oneness". This imaginative movement to form a oneness is especially transformative when we are able to make it with the self/other dichotomy. Identifying with the forest is such a movement, and the result is a transformative loss of one's 'me'. Imagined as integral to the whole, something of the fixed, insular nature of one's selfhood is lost. This is what (the imagined) Ziqi experienced.

Zhuangzi also makes clear that the loss of his 'me' does not entail the loss of his individuated experience of being an 'I'. Wang Fuzhi picks up on this: "[E]ach creature is 'I', for which reason nothing can be uniquely established as 'I'" (Ziporyn 2009; p 138). Each being is an "I", but in realizing this, no one "I" can remain sacrosanct; we are ushered into a higher view where the "I" has been equalized with every other "I". This is essentially something we were meant to learn in kindergarten, but Zhuangzi pushes it to its limits where it becomes a mystical experience. Wang continues: "Each creature is 'I'—the one who is capable of seeing it this way can only be called the Heavenly itself. Since every 'I' is then the Heavenly, to what opposite could I be coupled?" What he calls being the Heavenly, I call the view from Dao. To fully understand one's "I" as but one expression of infinite "I's" is to be loosed from the prison of that

"I"; the 'other' to which the "I" was coupled drops away and one experiences "a oneness", the Heavenly.

Zhuangzi is not saying that Ziqi took a walk in the woods where he lost his 'me', but because he chooses to describe that experience with reference to a forest, I follow that metaphor back into the woods. How then did he actually lose his 'me'? Zhuangzi is essentially mute on the subject, though some would have him engaging in traditional meditative practices. This is fine, according to our reading, as long as it doesn't import the typical metaphysical hocus-pocus that so often accompanies such advocacy. My sense, as already shared, is that here, as elsewhere, he suggests an imaginative exercise that might just as easily be called meditative.

Perhaps the most important benefit in understanding Ziqi's loss of his 'me' through the metaphor of the forest trees is that it keeps us in the world as we experience it. Zhuangzi's mysticism is not extra-mundane; it does not refer us to 'spiritual' realities beyond the possibilities of our everyday experience. In the text to follow, Zhuangzi will meet this issue head-on and declare that though some behind-the-scene Controller seems to be suggested by all this world-happening, it is only present as an absence, that is, "emptily so" (2:9). But he also says the same here: "We cannot discover a Who or What behind it" (2:6). Our task, therefore, is to explore the possibilities of our human experience within the boundaries of its givens.

Ziqi introduces his metaphor with reference to three kinds of "piping", those of man, earth and heaven. As things turn out, he advocates for the identification of the human piping with that of earth; we are invited to see the activities of humanity, especially its propensity to conjure up explanations of the world and to debate about them, as equivalent to the piping of the trees. They are all at some level the same and equal. This is meant to assist us to the realization of another point of view, one that shatters the shell of our self-absorption. It does not intend to suggest that we cannot then return to our explaining and debating—only now, we will not be so inclined to cling to them as to eternal truths, ideas worth fighting for. But what is the piping of heaven? asks his disciple. We do not know 'who' does the piping, is the reply. It seems to follow, however, that any and all piping is 'heaven's'. Apart from the relevance of our not-knowing-any-Doer to Ziqi's loss of 'me', no further relevance seems to be suggested here. Later, however, we will also be invited to emulate 'Heaven' itself (6:10), for this is ultimate rationale for *wuwei* and "not-being the change" (4).

TRANSCENDING THE HEART OF DUALISM

We have already discussed something of the nature of self as it manifests. Here I will add only that it is by nature an essentially dualistic experience. The self/other dichotomy is but an extension of the I/me dichotomy. Ziqi has lost "a part of himself", his "counterpart" or "partner" as some render it. Self-awareness is this I/me duality; without it, it is unlikely that there could be any self at all. But if this is the case, then Ziqi must in some sense have retained his 'me'. When he says 'I', it implies 'me'. When he speaks of the forest, he speaks of an 'other'. What has changed then, is his relationship to this self-experience.

We 'know' something only because we are able to see it as distinct from ourselves. We 'know' ourselves only because we relate to ourselves. Self is a relationship. Ziqi's experience is best understood, therefore, as the realization of a higher point of view that does not change the fundamental structure of the self-relationship, but rather puts in into a larger context, one that renders the otherwise insular "I" permeable and better able to identify with all other "I's". This conclusion may seem less than spectacular, but, as I have already said, Zhuangzi's "big words" are actually much more down-to-earth than we might immediately believe.

It might be argued that this separation from ourselves—for that is what the I/me dichotomy implies—is the cause of all our problems. Rocks do not experience despair; trees do not fear lightening; deer do not worry about the meaning of life and death. Yet, our self-conscious experience seems worth the price. And, in the final analysis, self-consciousness is what nature has wrought; it is our given. For Zhuangzi, what is given is to be affirmed and embraced; only he suggests that our relationship to these givens is mutable; we can, in non-dependence on them, transform our relationship to them. The self is not to be discarded, but more fully realized and enhanced in being transcended.

This is essential Zhuangzi; nothing of the human experience, even when in some way transcended, is ever abandoned or declared 'wrong'. No salvific or redemptive project is ever implied. Self, for all its problems and issues, is not vilified as an evil to be abrogated, but as something to be more fully realized. The Zhuangzian sage does not realize no-self, but rather no-fixed-self. The self remains as the seat of experience, only it now understands itself for the passing phenomenon that it is, and as such is able to more fully enjoy itself as a self. The sage has identified with the vastness in which things perpetually transform and all identity is momentary, and this enables the enjoyment of her present identity without the fear of its loss.

Here, the observation of the commentator Liu Xianxin (1896-1932) might be helpful: "The main principle of Buddhism is Emptiness; nothing is wanted; all is abandoned. The main principle of Daoism is vastness; everything is wanted; all is to be included" (Ziporyn; 2009, p 137). Though we need not press this distinction to the point of making these two approaches mutually exclusive, for they do in many ways complement each other, it does nonetheless illuminate what is distinctive of philosophical Daoism—its embrace of the entirety of the human experience and of fullness.

Once again, we see how the concept of Walking Two Roads helps to illustrate the simultaneous experiences of the transcendent and the mundane. We realize a sense of oneness, and informed by that sense, more fully realize the enjoyment of our individuality and uniqueness. We experience the loss of "me" in such a way as to be a happier "me".

Finally, we should not miss that all this discussion about self cannot be separated from the relationship between self and the world. Just as the 'me' is not eliminated, neither is the 'other'. Our engagement with the world is enhanced, not diminished. We are in the world, and Zhuangzi's vision is as much about how we might best transform and nurture that relationship as it is about the transformation and nurture of the self-relationship. In this regard, Wang Fuzhi is also able to tie Ziqi's experience into the overall theme of the chapter: "If you refrain from setting yourself up as the measure to be compared to the opposing counterpart, what theories of things, what assessments, are not made equal" (Ziporyn 2009; p 138)? Where all things and opinions are seen as equal, what need is there to impose one's own on others?

REFLECTIONS—PART TWO

THE HUMAN CONDITION

Having argued how we might attain a perspective that affirms all things, ourselves included, just as we are, skinny legs and all, Zhuangzi now proceeds to describe how messed up we actually are. This jaundiced view of the human condition could have been written by any one of a number of pessimistic philosophers of our own times. And this, to my thinking, gives us an inkling of how his suggested remedies might also be applicable to us today, despite having been written nearly two and a half millennia ago. Yet, in the end, Zhuangzi is no pessimist at all, but is rather so committed to the affirmation of all things that 'optimist', with its suggestion of its own opposite, cannot begin to encompass it. He thus describes the existential despair native to the human experience with a remedy in mind—though thankfully, in the end, no remedy is ultimately required. If one were indeed required, then all would not, in fact, be well. Still, there are possibilities for some palliative remedies, even if only approximately realized, and thus Zhuangzi sets the stage for his own. For, until we realize how sick we actually are, for all our supposed 'normalcy', we will seek no remedy at all. If, on the off-chance that the reader sees nothing of him- or herself in Zhuangzi's lament at the human condition, well, I think we can be confident that he would see no need to convince you otherwise. For he makes quite clear that he is describing his own experience and can only tentatively imply that it applies to others as well.

We might notice that Zhuangzi focuses his critique on the experience of the individual, not on political and social realities. There were, in his times too, certainly sufficiently horrible examples of human social dysfunction, injustice and suffering to occupy his thoughts should he have wished them to do so. This shift from the social to the individual is often cited by scholars as a significant innovation of Zhuangzi. We should not think, however, that he did not also have social harmony in mind. Only, he believed that the betterment of the world must begin with the betterment of the individual as we shall especially see in the fourth chapter. Our relationship with the world is determined by our relationship with ourselves.

Human beings, despite their hunger for purpose, meaning, and continuity, exist as if dangling over an empty void. This presents us with two fundamentally different possible responses; we can embrace this experience and formulate an authentic response to it, or we can attempt to fill that void with a theory intended to deny it. As a species, we almost universally default to the latter. But this, Zhuangzi tells us, simply leads to more suffering. Why? Because this 'dangle' is inherent and inescapable.

There are two ways by which we typically attempt to fill this void. First, we take our 'selves' as fixed-identities that will, or at least 'should', endure throughout all eternity. But this simply gives us something to lose and we are thus constantly fearful of its ending and of those unavoidable events that might contribute to the approach of that ending. Secondly, "we take our minds as our teachers" and devise theories about the world that attempt to explain away the 'dangle'. As we have seen, Zhuangzi sees the first of these as our core problem. Our dependence on being a concrete, fixed somebody simply exacerbates the problem. In actual experience 'we' are a becoming, not a fixed being; we are more human becomings than human beings. This becoming is not understood as entailing the continuity of one fixed identity through many transformations, but rather through the transformation of identities themselves through infinite identities. Harmonizing with this, we are able to release our fearful grip on life and follow along with the natural unfolding of the world-happening.

Our second attempted remedy is a consequence of the first. Wishing to preserve ourselves, we use our rationalizing minds to formulate theories that explain the world in such a way as to make it and our lives within it meaningful. Reason becomes our prop. But reason, for all its virtues, is "strangely unfixed" and has no foundation other than the one it imagines for itself, and is thus a flimsy reed upon which to lean. Kierkegaard describes this as sewing without a knot at the end of our thread; the activity of sewing becomes our *raison d'etre* while we ignore that it ever-unravels behind us.

Reason also serves to separate us from the world and ourselves. Whatever is thought is rendered an 'other'. Calling this tree a 'tree' is the objectification of this tree. The tree is now present as a representation of itself. Calling myself 'me', objectifies myself for myself and makes me not myself. This is the source of my experience of being 'dangled'. This is unavoidable, necessary and affirmable—it is to be a self. Only there are other more immediate ways in which to experience ourselves and the world, and Zhuangzi suggests that rather than being completely captivated by our reasoning minds, we instead trustingly surrender into the flow of life itself as something unexplained and unobjectified—as mystery (2:10).

BACK TO THE FOREST

In making his case for his proposed response to our existential dangle, Zhuangzi returns to the metaphor of the forest trees. If we had any doubt as to the relevance of the trees' piping (earth's piping) to our own, he here makes clear that all our activities, whether practical or emotive, inexplicably arise without any identifiable reason, as if out of a void, just as we more easily see with the trees (2:9). But this is offered as the cause of our sense of being tenuous, not as its remedy. The remedy follows in how we respond to this reality, and that requires returning to an appreciation of the equality of all things and theories. Take, for example, the chirping of baby birds (2:14). Do we believe that all our reasoned debate and profound theories about the world are different from the chirping of birds? They are; and we do. But are we also able to see how they are the same? If we have truly and deeply imagined this we will have broken through the shell of our burdensome sense of exceptionalism; we will have realized ourselves as momentary expressions of the great unfolding. Suddenly, everything is relativized. All those things to which we cling as to "eternal truths" (2:8), all our vexation about right and wrong (2:13), all our excessive seriousness—all these fall away, and with them, our sense of being a fixed-self. We are freed to wander in the harmony of every expression (5:4).

If the equalizing of human speech with the chirping of baby birds does not work for you, I would offer New York City. How does that city differ from a hive of bees? Or, more to the point, in what way is it the same? We needn't abandon what we take to be special about human material culture to realize that sense in which it is the same as and the absolutely equal to a hive of bees or a hill of ants; yet if we can manage it, our perspective on the human enterprise will be forever changed. The insular shell of our species-specific egoism and jingoism will be shattered. Suddenly the unnamable, mysterious Whole replaces our egoism with a vast openness. I say openness, because in mystery there is nothing upon which the mind can fix.

Part of the power of such imaginative exercises resides in the difficulties we discover in their attempt. They bring to the fore our innate prejudices. We can retain these if we feel we must, but at least we have had the opportunity to see them and in that to have come to know ourselves better. This, too, can be wandered in.

The "contending voices" of the trees (2:4) are representative of the debates of the philosophers, here the two leading contenders of Zhuangzi's time, the Confucians and the Mohists. As they negate each other with their various theories about how best to live, we too wish to join the fray and side with one or the other or to negate them both. But what happened to the view from Dao, asks Zhuangzi, that we would judge one dao right and another wrong (2:15)? Would we similarly judge between the chirpings of various birds or the sounds made by the trees in response to the wind? Isn't it the case that whatever we do is a dao, and that every dao is equally an expression of Dao? Return if we must to discriminating between them, but first let us realize the openness that obtains in seeing their sameness. Then, perhaps, we can wander unfettered and carefree among them.

ALL THINGS ARE ONE HORSE

We now enter what might be called the heart of Zhuangzi's logical argument. But if it is in fact an 'argument', is it not in at least two ways self-contradictory? If it is offered as an improvement upon the theories of the Confucians and Mohists, is it not really just one more theory and in that sense the same as theirs? It is. But unlike the Confucians and Mohists, whose theories negate that of the other, Zhuangzi's affirms them both, and every other theory, as well. And unlike these two, Zhuangzi offers his own argument in an upayic sense—it is not intended to represent how things 'really are', the truth, but rather to offer an imaginative exercise that might lead to a happier outcome. It is, in the end, only one suggested perspective that acknowledges that every perspective, even this one, is only that, and can never be a final word on anything.

The second sense in which we might see this argument as self-contradictory resides in its use of reason to make it. Hasn't he already demonstrated that reason cannot be relied upon to make sense of life? He has; but he never dismisses the use of reason as a legitimate human activity when it understands its own limits; and he does not transgress those limits here, since he makes no claims of 'knowing' anything. What to my thinking is more problematical is the possibility that we might take this reasoned argument as the basis for what must ultimately be a mystical experience, but this, from a Zhuangzian perspective, would be to "take our mind as our teacher" and thereby short-circuit the process at its inception. It would be to *depend on* something, in this case reasoned argument, and Zhuangzi's mystical vision is to experience what it is to depend on nothing, since nothing is in fact fixed and sure. Zhuangzi is aware of this, of course, and frequently implies that most everything he says is "reckless" and needs to be understood "recklessly" (2:37/54). He also informs us that none of the arguments made here can be 'applied' to facilitate his suggested outcome; this must happen "as a matter of course", that is, as something naturally arising in someone already mystically realized (2:24).

Zhuangzi's argument makes use of the subjective experience that says 'this' ('right'/ 'affirmable') of itself and 'that' ('wrong'/ 'unaffirmable') of what it objectifies to show how they can be united "to form a oneness". This sense of their oneness helps to facilitate an experience that relativizes and then subsumes our own subjectivity into a greater subjectivity, namely, the entirety of our world context as an open-ended unknowable. We are able to see the oneness of the forest, as well as the manyness of the trees (and ourselves among them), and this informs how we relate to the trees (and ourselves). As expressions of the forest, all the 'thises' and 'thats' of the trees are equalized. The forest is THIS, affirmable in its entirety, and the trees can thereby also be individually affirmed as THIS. In affirming the Whole, we affirm its every expression. "This can be called Dao as Convergence, the point of view that allows all daos to converge into a oneness. This point of view is like being at the center of a circle from which one can respond with equanimity to the endless parade of rights and wrongs that spin around one" (2:19). The realization of this view from Dao is the whole point of Zhuangzi's argument. Dao is all daos; all daos are Dao. This is their oneness. It is this "road" that Zhuangzi would have us realize so as to transform our relation to them in their more easily appreciated not-oneness.

The argument is made in several ways. Every 'that' that we posit is itself a 'this' that posits us as a 'that'. Every 'this' is also a 'that' and vice versa. Since we are simultaneously both, there is a sense in which they are both negated in us. This suggests a transcendent oneness, a higher category, a THIS that is the Whole. There being all these 'thises', moreover, we are led to ask if there is any one of them that can be said to be the one true and right 'this'. Since this exercise demonstrates at least some sense in which they are all equal—my 'me' being no more special than any other 'me'—we are able to understand our own subjectivity in the context of infinite subjectivities, thereby breaking down the insularity of our 'me'. It also seems that 'this' and 'that' require one another; 'thises' give rise to 'thats', and 'thats' give rise to 'thises'. Neither can exist without the other; they exist only as a oneness. They create each other. But by the same token, they also negate each other since every 'this' is also a 'that', and vice versa. Seeing 'this' and 'that' as such, we can unite them to form a oneness that equates to THIS.

Why THIS and not THAT? The word used here for 'this' (*shi*) also means 'right' and its opposite 'that' (*fei*) also means 'wrong'. Thus, through a bit of word play Zhuangzi is able to simultaneously make his case for the equalizing of the theories adhered to as 'right' or 'wrong' by all the 'thises' and 'thats'. Every act of 'this-ing' is an assertion of affirmability, of rightness. Zhuangzi affirms all things and their theories, not necessarily in their factual accuracy, but in that they are all equally expressions of the world-happening just as the "contending voices" of the forest's trees are equally expressions of the forest. Taking all expressions as THIS is affirming all things.

Zhuangzi's use of the arguments of the logician Gongsun Long (2:20) are the subject of much debate, not only in what that use intends to say, but also in what Long himself intended to say, and whether that has any logical validity. I have made my best effort in my adaptation to express Zhuangzi's use (which likely made free with whatever point Long wished to make), but cannot vouch for its accuracy. I would be tempted to pass over this section if it were not for his dramatic conclusions—"Heaven and earth are one finger. All things are one horse." The logicians were concerned with the limitations of language to accurately represent the world, demonstrated these though paradoxes, threw up their hands, and left it at that. Zhuangzi essentially agrees with them, but sees this discovery as an invitation to go beyond language and return to our embedding in the inexplicable Whole from which language can only provisionally and inaccurately attempt to slice off bits. If we can understand that sense in which "all things are one horse" we will have understood his point.

Long used 'this' particular white horse to argue that because it is white it does not belong to the category 'horse' which does not include whiteness. Zhuangzi suggests that we instead use 'that' horse to show that 'this' horse is not a horse, just as he has shown that 'this' and 'that' cancel out each other. And, just as that mutual-sublimation leads to an affirmable oneness, a THIS, so also does this procedure lead us to HORSE. "All things are one horse."

Though he does not further explore it, there is also the possibility that Zhuangzi is opening us up to what Ziporyn calls "omnicentrism" (Ziporyn 2004; pp 82ff). Not only are the many parts of the Whole, but every part is itself the Whole. Every individual thing is both the center and the periphery. Every 'thing' is Everything. 'Horse' explains Everything. But then, so too does 'cow'. I will leave the readers to explore this further should they wish.

REFLECTIONS—PART THREE

TRANSCENDING RIGHT AND WRONG

As previously stated, the power of Zhuangzi's suggestion that we equalize right and wrong lies as much in our resistance to doing so as in the consequence of our accomplishing it. The proof of our bondage to such discriminations is here made abundantly clear. Yet, he is not in fact discounting the legitimacy of such discriminations, but only wishes to show that they are merely a human invention and that they are ultimately perspectivally derived. Because they are not written in heaven, does not mean that they have no validity. They are, however, only a matter of perspective, and though we tend to agree that 'murder', for instance, is wrong, we do not agree on what constitutes murder. One person's murder is another's justice. "Collateral damage" in the killing of "suspected terrorists" is perfectly legitimate for some and murder for others. So, Zhuangzi might ask, is there murder or is there no murder?

Just as we saw that the equalizing of 'this' and 'that' leads Zhuangzi to affirm all things as THIS, so also does equalizing right and wrong lead to an affirmation of all things as RIGHT. Because the Whole is RIGHT (affirmable), so too are all its manifestations. All things are right and affirmable because they exist. This is their oneness. But they also have their not-oneness, and as human beings we must address this in the context of that oneness.

Zhuangzi's objective is not to make us amoral (or immoral!), but to help us to experience a sense of our fundamental embedding in the Whole in which no such discriminations exist. In this he is by no means unique. The first extant Zen document, the *Xin-Xin Ming* says the same: "The Great Way [Dao] is not difficult for those not attached to preferences" (Clarke, 1970).

The 24th verse provides us with important clarifications of Zhuangzi's dao. First, he tells us that understanding what he has said about uniting opposites to form a oneness is possible only after one has experienced it. This makes clear that our point of entry is not through logical argument but that this comes only after the fact. Secondly, he tells us that this dao is not the 'right' dao relative to other daos, one that judges the rightness or wrongness of other daos so as to 'correct' them, but rather that it affirms them all just as they are. Thus, were someone to call his dao 'wrong', Zhuangzi would affirm that from that point of view it is. Finally, he tells us that a sage does not practice this dao because it is 'right', but because it has become her nature to do so. In this we begin to see the sage as a singularly receding figure, an embodiment of *wuwei*, instead of a charismatic guru lording over others. Dao, it turns out, is simply letting all things be themselves.

WALKING TWO ROADS

Only now does Zhuangzi introduce this important trope of walking two roads, though I have already made repeated reference to it since, in its simplicity, it so adequately clarifies his point of view. I have, admittedly, applied it more generally and in different contexts than he, but without, I believe, in any way compromising his intended meaning here (2:27). In a nutshell, walking two roads suggests that we can simultaneously participate in two points of view, the view from Dao, a 'higher', more transcendent perspective, and the view from humanity, a more circumspect perspective. The view from Dao is to "understand the piping of Heaven"; the view from humanity is to "understand the piping of earth and man" (2:2). One does not supersede the other, but since the view from Dao is not our default perspective and is remedial, it becomes necessary to prioritize it so as to allow it to inform our 'normal' everyday perspective. Contrasting examples of these two points of view are: the amorality of Nature versus the morality of humanity; the 'all is well' of the Whole versus the dysfunction of humanity; the indifference of Nature versus the caring of humanity; the goodness of death versus the desire to live; the happiness that depends on nothing versus the happiness that depends on circumstances. In each case, the human is affirmed while opened-up into the freedom of the all-affirming Totality.

Zhuangzi introduces this concept through the parable of the monkey trainer whose monkeys fail to realize that 3+4=4+3. To realize how that nothing is lost however things are arranged is the view from Dao, and this the trainer realizes. But rather than needing to convince the monkeys of this, the trainer, because he understands it, can simply follow along with the monkey's 'this/right'. Thus does the trainer simultaneously walk two roads.

This view that understands how nothing can be lost however arranged when hidden in the Whole, becomes an important component of Zhuangzi's remedy for the fear of death later in the text (6:9).

Zhuangzi actually introduces this parable to demonstrate the folly of trying to prove that all things are 'one', since whatever view we hold, things are as they are in any case. Arguments for or against oneness are like those between advocates for 3+4 against advocates for 4+3; they are, in any event, the same and equal. The trees might debate whose response to the wind is best, but the forest embraces them all equally; every expression is 'right'.

REFLECTIONS—PART FOUR

THE WANING OF DAO

Zhuangzi continues his critique of language and the bifurcating discriminations to which it gives rise by way of a mythological history of the devolution of our sense of oneness, the view from Dao. I have taken the liberty of introducing this bit of fantasy as a self-aware fabrication since we seem to need constant reminders that Zhuangzi, despite the seriousness of his project, is also having fun. His meta-message that our non-dependence on any message releases us to playfully enjoy life is always present in and as his medium.

This devolution of our sense of Dao in four stages parallels the evolution of human self-consciousness and the accumulation of knowledge that accompanies it. The ancients are represented as 'having the Dao' in that they understood that they understood nothing, there being nothing to understand. This primitivist concept is an important one in Daoism and for this reason is often presented in the extreme. The *Laozi* tells us that those who seek knowledge increase in it day by day, while those who seek Dao decrease in knowledge day by day (68). The real problem with knowledge and the rational mind that pursues it is that it becomes so enamored of itself that it knows no other way of being in the world. One's integration with the larger context of the utterly unknowable is lost, and this is the source of our deep sense of alienation. It is re-integration with this to which Daoism appeals. This unknowable context is Mystery, the uncarved block, chaos, Dao. If one attempts this re-integration by way of knowledge or technique, this is simply more of the same. For this reason, I believe, Zhuangzi's ultimate appeal is to a mystical movement that I describe as trustful surrender into what is in any case unavoidable.

Reason and the accumulation of knowledge are natural and wonderful human endowments and should be allowed to flourish to their fullest—within their natural limits. "Therefore, when the rationalizing mind restfully settles in what it cannot know, it has fully realized itself" (2:44). Many of the assumptions of science and most the pronouncements of religion transgress these limits. Zhuangzi picks up this theme again in the opening lines of the sixth chapter.

These "ancients" can be understood as having the view from Dao which means that they are obliged to have a perspective—they are not themselves "the uncarved block", but have an awareness of it. They are obliged to walk two roads. The devolution of Dao has already begun in them, but this is the price of self-consciousness, a price we gladly pay.

The central theme here is that the more we divide up the world through our discriminating consciousness, the further removed from it we become. Thus, the devolution of Dao is seen as a progressive cutting up of experience. There are things, but no clear borders between them. Then there are clear borders. And finally, we judge between them, deeming some things better and more worthy than others. This is the source of our inherent alienation from ourselves and the world that Zhuangzi earlier described and seeks to remedy. "When rights and wrongs waxed bright and completely defined how we see the world, the view from Dao waned and grew dim. This loss of the view from Dao is precisely what caused the ceaseless disquiet seen in our need to cling to some things while rejecting others and in our constant worry about benefit and harm, gain and loss" (2:32).

Ah, but Zhuangzi never leaves things so formulaically simple. Yes, there is a sense in which we can say that Dao waned, but are we in fact justified in *discriminating* between waxing and waning? We are, and we are not—there are two roads to walk here as well. Implied here, I believe, though Zhuangzi does not explicate it, is that there is a psychological Dao which can be 'lost' or 'attained' and a metaphysical Dao that cannot be either lost or attained. This parallels not-one also being One (6:7). Metaphysical Dao refers to the uncarved block, the Whole, the Mystery, that makes no discrimination between things. Psychological Dao is our appreciation of this and can wax or wane. Shendao, a 'legalist' and to my thinking proto-Daoist philosopher of Zhuangzi's time, is quoted as having said "a clump of earth never strays from the Dao" (33; Ziporyn 2009; p122). This clump necessarily participates in metaphysical Dao—the "Great Clump"—as do we; the difference is that we, being self-aware (inherently dualistic beings), are also required to psychologically realize this, and this is the view from Dao.

Zhuangzi's actual demonstration of how waxing and waning can be united to form a oneness uses something much more humanly immediate, our sense of success and failure. He introduces three historical examples (though he only discusses two) of men who were apparent successes, yet can be seen in the retrospect of a larger context to have been failures. The famous zither player Zhen Wen's accomplishments seem to dissolve when his son cannot match them—his talent was lost forever. Huizi's writings "filled five carts" (33), but are all now lost; though famous in his time as a great debater, what did it all amount to? Is it not obvious that whatever success a human being might achieve in life, it is ultimately negated in death? This is simply an acknowledgement of the overarching sense of futility that characterizes the human experience, however 'successful' any one life might appear to be or have been.

If, however, we take the view from Dao that understands how these apparent successes and failures are all equal happenings within the Great Happening, then they all can be seen as SUCCESSES. When 'this' and 'that' are united to form a oneness, every expression becomes THIS, affirmable. When right and wrong are so united, every expression becomes RIGHT simply by virtue of its having arisen. So too is every relative human success or failure ultimately a SUCCESS simply in having succeeded in expressing a dao where every dao is Dao. Imagine the greatest human success story and the greatest story of human failure—they are equally SUCCESS. We might think this simply provides a way out for the greatest 'failures' among us, but as we saw earlier in Zhuangzi's critique of the human condition, the greatest 'successes' among us equally suffer from a profound sense of the ultimate futility of every human endeavor.

This equalizing perspective is similarly revealed in Huizi's paradoxical pronouncement quoted a bit further along: "No one lives longer than a dead child, and Pengzu [who lived for hundreds of years] died young (2:39)!" In Dao, all things are equalized and equally affirmed. In Dao, all is well.

"Thus does the sage aim for the realization of a profound radiance in the equalizing submergence of all human activity. She does not make fixed judgments about things, but just lets them be what they are. This again is shining the light of the obvious to show the equality of things" (2:35). This "radiance" is carefree joy.

THE ILLUMINATION OF THE OBVIOUS

Several times in this chapter Zhuangzi speaks of "shining the light of the obvious" on things to reveal their oneness in their sameness (2:16, 19, 35). This is *yiming*, which simply means to illuminate or illumination. Ziporyn translates "Illumination of the Obvious" which he admits is controversial (Ziporyn; 2009, pp 217-8). I have followed him, though I have de-mystified it a bit in removing the uppercase. The uppercase is not altogether unjustified, however, since Zhuangzi does seem to present it as an actual and important exercise to be employed. Many, again of a more religious mind, take it to be descriptive of an experience of enlightenment wherein one realizes the Truth. Ziporyn correctly, I believe, sees this as negating Zhuangzi's fundamental point of departure, namely that knowledge cannot penetrate mystery and we are thus obliged to let it remain as such. The Illumination of the Obvious is thus simply the exercise of a commonsense and honest evaluation of things as they appear to be. This I call a phenomenological approach (though an actual phenomenologist might disagree) in that it describes experience rather than explains it. Curiously, this use of commonsense seems to turn what we usually view as commonsense on its head. We believe we are 'someone', for instance, as a matter of commonsense, but further inquiry demonstrates that we have *added* this to the mix—we cannot in fact find any 'someone' there. We think that commonsense shows that right and wrong are written in heaven, but a bit more illumination shows that this cannot be supported by the evidence. Zhuangzi's commonsense is, in the end, a commonsense critique of what we erroneously take to be commonsense. What Zhuangzi is saying here, and throughout the presentation of his vision is: Get real. Be honest. That's the way to live authentically.

ONE PLUS WORDS EQUALS TWO

Zhuangzi next demonstrates how words are inherently inadequate in their attempts to make sense of the world. Yet, since he is required to use them to make his case against their hegemony, he asks our indulgence, and thereby walks two roads.

When we declare everything THIS, words naturally understand it in counter-distinction to something else, a THAT. But that is not the Zhuangzian THIS—something that can only be experienced, and never said (2:35). Everything said is an act of distinguishing something in contrast to something else; every coherence has its background incoherence; every attempt at inclusion results in the exclusion of something else (2:42). Words are necessarily dualistic in that they always also imply what they are not (to say 'horse' is to also say 'not-cow') and in that they always leave out what cannot be articulated, and this latter is, for Daoism, always the most important thing of all *because* it has been left out. Without it, there is no sense of oneness.

Through an argument of infinite regress in the pursuit of an absolute beginning, an arising of existence from out of non-existence, Zhuangzi demonstrates yet another limitation of reason (2:37-8). However much it knows, it cannot know the essential.

He next quotes some paradoxes posed by his friend Huizi as valid responses to this inadequacy of words (2:39). They attempt to force us into a *commonsense* acknowledgement of the ultimate equality of all things that relativizes all the distinctions we make between them. Many commentators see his presentation of these as ridicule, citing his following argument against the definitive pronouncement of Oneness. I disagree, and have framed them as affirmed. Of course they fall short and contain within them their own self-contradiction, just as Zhuangzi acknowledges that all *his* words fall short and are self-contradictory.

The first two of these paradoxes play upon the relative comparatives of size and duration. The tip of an autumn hair is clearly smaller than Mt. Tai, but is there a context in which they can be seen as equal? If so, we could just as easily interchangeably declare them both superlatively the smallest and the biggest—not because they are, but because neither the comparative nor the superlative any longer has applicable meaning at all. The author of the 17th chapter, who was likely a disciple of Zhuangzi, makes much of the relative nature of such discriminations and would argue here that Mt. Tai, for instance, might be bigger that the tip of an autumn hair, but since it is also smaller than something else, is both bigger and smaller. Thus, we cannot describe it as either. There is always something comparatively bigger, smaller, longer, shorter, older, younger. This argument, though of interest, is not strictly speaking that of Zhuangzi. This author is much more rationally inclined than Zhuangzi and appears to believe he can reason his way into a sense of oneness. However, I believe Zhuangzi offers these paradoxes here as puzzles that reason cannot solve, very much like a Zen koan. The point is not to 'figure them out', but to experience something that reason cannot frame. They are intended to push us into an experiential inkling of the "uncarved block" where no such discriminations abide.

Equalizing the life experience of a dead (perhaps stillborn) child and Pengzu (the Chinese Methuselah) is especially powerful, touching as it does on our most precious experience, life itself. "No one lives longer than a dead child." Where does our imagination have to go to appreciate this? It requires us to in some sense devalue what we value most. It pushes us into an affirmation of the vastest arrangement where nothing is ever lost, where a long life and a short life have no meaning at all. Zhuangzi will later describe the outcome of this realization in the attitude of a sage: "Premature death, long life, our beginning and our ending, the sage sees them all as equivalent and good" (6:10). This attitude, however, is the fruit of an experience, and that is what this paradox is intended to facilitate.

This radical devaluation of the duration of the life experience also provides us with an excellent example of what it means to walk two roads. For Zhuangzi often tells us that one of the most practical benefits of following this dao is that we will "fully live out our allotted years" (1:24, 2:58, 3:1, 4:19, 6:1). We fully value life for all it can be and seek its flourishing in every possible way, yet whatever transpires can be embraced with equanimity when all is understood in the context of that from which nothing can ever be lost or diminished. This is to walk two roads.

For many commentators, taking the last of these paradoxes as affirmed borders on heresy. "Heaven, earth and I were born at the same moment, and I and everything else make One!" If we were to take this as a declaration of fact, then it would indeed be heretical from a Zhuangzian perspective. However, if we understand it as a paradox comparable to those that have preceded it, then we can see how it descriptive of an experience, not a statement of fact. Having eliminated all distinctions, Zhuangzi makes this ecstatic declaration not because he believes it true of the world, but because he has experienced an inexplicable sense of oneness.

This paradox is usually attributed to Huizi like the previous two; but I'm not so sure. He too arrived at a sense of oneness, but apparently only logically so. We find his comparable statement in the 33rd chapter: "Love all things without exception, for heaven and earth are one body" (Ziporyn; p 124). My sense is that Zhuangzi followed Huizi to this same conclusion, but for him it became a mystical experience, rather than a logical conclusion. Thus, I take this as Zhuangzi's own ecstatic exclamation.

This seems a good place to once again attempt a clarification of Zhuangzi's position on Oneness. He never definitively declares there is a One—something that he next demonstrates as absurd in as much as saying there is One divides it in two. In addition, to definitively posit a One would be to *depend on* a belief in something. For Zhuangzi, even a belief in 'God' would be an obstacle to freedom since the most obvious thing about us is that we have-no-clue about anything. What he does believe is that Oneness seems to be indicated though we cannot genuinely imagine or articulate it. But this inexplicability, this doubt, is for him an invitation to mystically open himself up into it—not as something known, but as something unknown. This experience does not require that there be One, and is not envisioned as some form of redemptive realization, but is purely remedial, palliative, upayic, and provisional. It is simply making the best possible use of the useless, our inescapable not-knowing.

THE DARK BRILLIANCE

"Therefore, when the rationalizing mind restfully settles in what it cannot know, it has fully realized itself. The proof that uses no words, the Dao that is not-a-dao—who can 'know' them? The ability to in some sense 'understand' these I call tapping the Heavenly Reservoir. It is poured into, but never full, partaken of, but never emptied. Yet we are ever-not-knowing from whence it comes. It is simply life itself. Let's call it The Dark Brilliance" (2:44-5). This is the frontier, the very edge, of Zhuangzi's mystical vision—and necessarily leaves us with no clear next step. Having understood that our understanding cannot re-integrate us with the world, life, or ourselves, we are invited to try another approach. Zhuangzi gives this movement no name—I describe it as a thankful surrender in trust into things as they 'are'. This is the simplest (and hardest) thing possible, and while no 'answer' at all, is the only authentic one provided us.

What is this Heavenly Reservoir? Ziporyn suggests it is the mind of the sage (2009; p 17, note 23). Though it certainly includes the mind of the sage, I have suggested that it is "life itself", but this too is inseparable from the Mystery of the upwelling of everything. Re-integration with one's life is re-integration with Mystery. Where all is Mystery, everything is mystery, and surrender into mystery is surrender into Mystery. Thus, though much has been said about metaphysical Dao as the unknowable Totality, Zhuangzi suggests that we do have a point of psychological experiential entry in our experience of life itself. How could it be otherwise? There is nothing closer or more immediate than our life experience—this alone we can experience without first making it some 'other'. Ultimately, Zhuangzi's vision is for our re-integration (a realization of a sense of belonging in oneness) with Mystery through the gate of our own mysterious life experience. If we can say Yes to ourselves, we will have said Yes to everything else.

What is The Dark Brilliance? It is the entirety of our interface with everything. It is our life experience. All is Mystery—unknowable, ungrounded, unexplained, seemingly meaningless, purposeless—Dark. Yet, out of this arises life and its affirming joy—a Brilliance. It is the "usefulness of the useless". It is yang emerging from yin. It is the joyful experience of "tapping into the Heavenly Reservoir" though we are "ever-not-knowing its Source".

REFLECTIONS—PART FIVE

LET TEN THOUSAND FLOWERS BLOOM

The chapter closes with five vignettes that help to illustrate the perspectives shared above. The first of these is a parody of a story related in the later Han syncretistic document the *Huainanzi* (c. 140 B.C.E.) In that story ten suns rose and withered all the crops and thus Yao ordered nine shot out of the sky. The metaphor is intended to convey the need for one sole ruler as the best way for the world to be managed. By extension, there should also be only one dao, one true way, one Truth. Zhuangzi, however, turns this completely on its head and has Shun suggest that, to the contrary, the more daos the better. Ziporyn puts it succinctly: "Yao thinks ten different standards of 'rightness' will lead to chaos—there must be a single unified truth, a single ruler. Zhuangzi here allows all things their own rightness—and thereby there will be all the more illumination, with each thing its own sun" (2009; p17, note 24).

PERSPECTIVAL RELATIVISM

This next story is an important one in that it further illustrates the nature of Zhuangzi's skepticism. Wang Ni, an ostensible sage, is interviewed by Toothless regarding what he knows. This turns out to be nothing, and most importantly for those who concern themselves with degrees and species of skepticism, he does not even know whether he knows or doesn't know anything.

Still, he at least knows what has led him to his skepticism, namely that all our determinations about what is 'best' are perspectively derived. Eels like it cold and clammy; people like it warm and cozy. Who are we to say that one is right and the other wrong? All definitions of what is right and what is wrong are so hopelessly tangled he cannot sort them out. Toothless predictably protests that in that case Wang Ni cannot even distinguish between what is beneficial for him and what is harmful, though this does not necessarily follow; Wang Ni provisionally knows what's beneficial for him—he's just not going to impose that on anyone else or worry overmuch if he gets it wrong. Nevertheless, Wang shifts the discussion to the 'higher' road; on that road, the sage does not worry about benefit and harm because ultimately she fears nothing that may transpire since she takes even life and death as equal. There is ultimately nothing she can lose.

I have taken the liberty to rephrase the text where it says more literally, for instance, that the lakes might burn, but the sage is not burned with them. This hyperbole is too easily taken by the religious mind as a miraculous quality of the sage, when Zhuangzi clearly had no such claim in mind. She would indeed be burned, and would wisely avoid being burnt should she be able; only whether burned on not, she thankfully follows along with the unavoidable without fear.

AWAKENING TO THE DREAMING

The third story is packed with important insights. One of the more novel of these is the censure of an over-zealous disciple for his belief in the standard description of the fantastic attributes of a sage. It is not that that description is incorrect, but that clinging to it as if to some fixed goal effaces the true spirit of sagacity. It's a bit like the Zen declaration: If you meet the Buddha, kill him! Trying to 'become' a buddha defeats any chance of becoming one. Wanting to be a sage is wanting to be someone special, and this is the antithesis of the heart of sagacity which is to be no one special, and the best way to accomplish this is to thoroughly affirm who you are—just as you are. The attributes of a sage flow from who she is; to seek them for oneself before becoming a sage is to put the cart before the horse.

Still, there is a paradoxical dialectic at play here; descriptions of sagacity *can* be helpful, just as words, though they always miss the mark and can distract from that to which they point, are nonetheless required. Thus High Tree, the sage, proposes to speak "recklessly" provided that his disciple similarly listens "recklessly". So also, I believe, would Zhuangzi have us understand these Inner Chapters as having been written recklessly, in the hope that we would read them recklessly. The alternative is to take them all very seriously, to take them as describing some fixed and 'true' dao to follow. His central theme of non-dependent wandering would be self-defeating if we depended on its realization. For philosophical Daoism, what isn't self-effacing, is self-defeating (2:43).

Here also is an important clarification of the scope of Zhuangzi's vision through the metaphor of dreaming. As self-conscious beings we are forever at work trying to make sense of our life experience, but since we are ourselves utterly a-dangle—ungrounded in anything fixed and sure—all this conscious experience is comparable to a dreaming. Zhuangzi suggests we awaken *to* that dreaming, but does not suggest that we can awaken *from* the dreaming. We are used to more religious presentations of this metaphor where we awaken from our dreaming to a realization of Truth, Reality, Universal Mind, or some other absolute. This amounts to an interpretation of the dream within the dream. Zhuangzi is far less ambitious; it is enough for him to realize that we are dreaming and in that to make the best use of it. Never does he propose salvation from our inherent not-knowing, our dreaming. His remedy is purely palliative, an open-ended opening into Openness, which is to say, into Mystery.

In this context, Zhuangzi once again points to the folly of seeking for or following after sages. If surrender into Mystery is the best we can do, what point would there be in waiting for someone to come along and supposedly explain it all away? And why would we believe them in any case? Would it not simply lead to more endless debate? Even the sages disagree with each other's interpretations of the dream (within the dream); how can we choose between them? We would be better off just enjoying the dream and tinkering with it so as to enable us to more fully do so.

Finally, Zhuangzi incongruously (recklessly!) has his character refer back to his own opening metaphor of the contending voices of the trees in response to the wind. These debaters think they are sorting out right and wrong interpretations of the world, but each one is already 'right' from his own perspective. They seem to depend upon each other for the discovery of what is 'right', but since each one is already right from his own perspective, this apparent mutual dependence is in fact non-dependence (Ziporyn 2009; p 20, note 24).

UNIVERSAL MUTUAL-DEPENDENCE EQUALS NON-DEPENDENCE

This theme of non-dependence arising out of total universal mutual-dependence is next taken up in Penumbra's conversation with Shadow. A penumbra is that area of diffused shadow that surrounds a more defined shadow. In Zhuangzi's time, it was a mythical creature said to be the shadow of a shadow. According to Ziporyn, the character means literally, "the neither of the two" (2009; p 20, note 36) which evokes the theme of walking two roads, the transcending of opposites through an embracing of both, in this case, dependence and independence in the realization of non-dependence. When dependence is coupled with its opposite, independence, then one must be the case and the other not; but when these two "open into each other" the result is, like Penumbra, "the neither of the two". And this is Zhuangzi's non-dependence.

Penumbra, the shadow of Shadow, asks why Shadow's behavior seems so erratic. Shadow replies that he does not know why he is so, but this doesn't apparently matter in terms of his sense of freedom. Whether wholly dependent on things external to himself or not, freedom to wander as a psychological orientation is always possible. Indeed, Zhuangzian 'soaring' *requires* obstacles to freedom to realize freedom. We can be free even if utterly determined. We can wander in non-dependence even when totally dependent.

Ironically, Penumbra, who must be mirroring Shadow's behavior, only questions Shadow's independence—apparently, he's thoroughly convinced of his own. Shadow is more insightful and wonders whether whatever he depends on does not depend on something else, and that on something else, *ad infinitum*. All things are ultimately universally mutually-dependent, but if we take this as a totality and identify with it as such, upon what do we or it depend? This is the non-dependent freedom that arises when we release ourselves into the ever-transforming—our own transforming in this present identity and on into the next is not the loss of something, but rather a participation in everything.

If we turn and consider our own shadow we are likely to think it is entirely dependent on us and ourselves as independent. But our shadow, were it able, would also probably think the same of itself relative to us and its penumbra. Are we really any different than these? If there is a shadow, is there a sense in which it is as full and real as ourselves? If all things and theories can be equalized, then so also can I and my shadow. My shadow is as 'real' and as affirmable as I. When Ziqi lost his 'me', his sense of being an isolated someone, his present identity though presently persisting and affirmed, also became permeable with every other identity and was happily recognized as only a "temporary lodging". Non-dependence also entails no need to be 'me'. This sense of the unfixity of identity is the theme of the concluding story of this chapter, the famous Butterfly Dream.

THE TRANSFORMATIONS OF IDENTITY

Perhaps the most popularly celebrated of Zhuangzi's stories is the Butterfly Dream that closes this chapter. Zhuangzi so vividly dreams he is a butterfly that upon awakening he is not sure whether he is Zhuangzi who has dreamt he was a butterfly or a butterfly now dreaming he is Zhuangzi. Superficially, we might assume that he is either one or the other. But if it is *all* a dream, then the one is as valid as the other, and 'Zhuangzi' is both, either and neither. The point of the story is found in its own self-interpretation: "Clearly, these are two distinct identities. This is what can be called transformation—one's present identity being only a temporary lodging" (2:61). Our difficulty in understanding the story arises from our inability to think outside the confines of a fixed-identity. We believe that there is one identity in play, even if it transforms from one manifestation into another. This came up earlier in our discussion of the popular understanding of the "transmigration of souls", re-incarnation. It is believed that there is a fixed, core identity, a 'soul', that re-manifests in a variety of forms. But Zhuangzi's idea is much more radical than this; identities, though real enough at the time of their expression, are themselves as transitory as the forms they take. There is a sense in which 'I' become something else, but the same 'I' no longer has a place in it. Identity itself, not its form, is a "temporary lodging". A temporary lodging for what? Just as thought requires the artificial reality of words, so also imagining this "what?" requires the artificial reality of identity. We simply cannot imagine any reality without its having an identity.

This same idea is addressed again in the 6th chapter where we are told: "We inexplicably discover ourselves involved in the experience of being human and then assign ourselves a concrete identity and call it 'myself'. But how do we know that this self-identity has any reality to it? If you dream you are a bird, you think yourself a bird-identity and fly; if you dream you are a fish, you think yourself a fish-identity and swim. Might not I now be dreaming I'm a human-identity and thus do the human thing? When we laugh, it is spontaneous and not because we have carefully reasoned things out; so too with being human. When you understand your present 'identity' in the context of the ever-transforming, no matter what that present 'identity' might be, and yet fully embrace it and play within it as a unique and distinct expression, then you experience the obvious oneness of Nature" (6:30-1).

CHAPTER THREE

A WAY OF FLOURISHING

THE TEXT

THE IMPORTANCE OF NOURISHING LIFE

1 Life flows within limiting banks; human speculation, on the other hand, goes wherever it likes. If life is forced to follow after the unknowable, it is harmed. If, knowing this, one still seeks what cannot be known, life is harmed all the more. Left to follow its own course, life may do 'good', but not in such a way as to gain reputation; or it may do 'evil', but not in such a way as to bring punishment. Life flows within us, and left to follow its own course, our bodies will be maintained, our life allowed to flourish, our loved-ones nourished, and our allotted years realized.

2 A cook was butchering an ox for King Hui of Wei. The swing of his arms, the movement of his shoulders, the placing of his feet, the swish of his knife—all these were done as if performing a ritual dance.

3 Watching him, the king exclaimed, "Such skill is truly remarkable!" But the cook put down his knife and said, "Sir, your servant rather follows Dao, which is beyond mere skill. When I first began butchering oxen, for three years all I could see was one big ox without knowing much about it. But now I see oxen with my spirit rather than solely with my eyes. My rational mind no longer imposes itself on the oxen and my spirit's natural impulses take over. Thus do I discover the natural boundaries and cut as though through huge seams and wide hollows. I follow the way oxen actually are and thus never hit a ligament or tendon, much less a bone."

4 "A skillful cook must replace his blade every year, since it gets chipped. An unskilled cook has to replace his knife every month, since it gets broken. Your servant, however, has been using this same knife for nineteen years and has butchered thousands of oxen, and yet it is still as sharp as when it left the grindstone."

5 "For even the joints have tiny spaces between them, and my knife seems to have no thickness. Having no thickness, my knife finds a vast space to play its way through them. This is how it has remained sharp for so long."

6 "Still, sometimes I encounter a spot so tricky that its severing seemingly cannot be done. It is then that, slowing down and seeing nothing, I let the knife move as if of itself. Suddenly, the ox has undone itself and the piece falls to the ground with a thud! And I, well I savor the moment with pleasure, carefully clean the blade and put it away."

7 At this the king exclaimed, "This is wonderful! My lowly cook has shown me how to nourish my life!"

8 When Gongwen Xuan met the Commander of the Right he was amazed. "You have only one leg!" he exclaimed. "Is this a consequence of human activity or did it happen naturally?" The Commander replied, "It's natural, of course. Whenever nature does something it is always as a unique 'This'. Human beings, however, always need to pair things with a 'that'—everything has to be put into a mental box, 'this' is natural 'that' is not. Thus, however I came to have only one leg, it happened naturally because it is so."

9 The marsh pheasant must take ten steps to find a morsel, and a hundred steps to get a drink. Yet it would prefer to live like this than to live in a cage and be fed and watered like a king—at the cost of a fettered spirit.

10 When Lao Dan died, Qin Shi went to his wake only to abruptly and indecorously depart. One of Lao Dan's disciples caught up with him and said, "Weren't you a friend of the Master!?" "I was," replied Qin. "Then was that the proper way to mourn him!?" retorted the disciple. "Indeed, it was!" answered Qin. "When I came to the wake I expected to find those

who embodied Lao's teaching, but instead I found a bunch of bawling sycophants crying as if for a lost son or mother. Whether Lao was to blame for this or not, I cannot say; but in any case, clearly his teaching failed to take root. Fearful that I too might get caught up in such foolishness, I left. For to so mourn would have been to forget life as received, to flee from reality, and to oppose what is natural. Long ago they called this excessive sorrow the punishment for fleeing reality."

11 "When the time came to arrive, the Master arrived; when it was time to leave, he left. He followed the natural course of things, so that the joy and sorrow that depends on circumstances could not enter his heart. Long ago they called this being freed from the dangle of a tenuous existence."

12 We can only see what happens to the firewood; we cannot see what becomes of the fire.

REFLECTIONS

FOLLOWING THE FLOW OF LIFE

The title to this chapter tells us that nourishing our inner lives is the most important thing we can do. Everything else flows from this. Self-cultivation may appear to some to be an individualistic indulgence in egoism, but from the point of view of philosophical Daoism it is what makes the betterment of our social and environmental contexts most effective, though it is not pursued for this reason.

Zhuangzi begins with a statement of his fundamental insight into the human experience: Life flows within banks, its insurmountable givens, while the mind relentlessly overflows those banks in search of what life itself does not and cannot provide, namely fixed and sure guarantees of purpose, meaning and continuity. The result is inner disharmony and alienation. The previous chapter illustrated the futility of this endeavor by way of a critique of reason and language. There, he concluded that the mind is most fulfilled when it realizes its limitations and rests within them (2:44). Failure to do this equates, he later says, to "adding to the process of life" (5:18). This is "taking one's mind as one's teacher" and the alternative is to follow the flow of life itself—but what does this mean?

The celebrated story, shortly to follow, of the cook butchering an ox goes a long way in illustrating this for us, but still it remains within the medium of metaphor and we are thus left to figure it out for ourselves. Clearly, some form of spontaneous living is implied. This concept is never directly addressed by Zhuangzi, but always only implied. In this immediate context it suggests that the mind not be allowed to mediate between oneself and one's life; we do not act because we have determined that it is the 'best' course of action, but because this is how life itself expresses itself. This is seen in the sage who affirms all expressions, not because she deems it the 'right' thing to do, but rather "as a matter of course" (2:24). "Taking one's mind as one's teacher" is thus the antithesis of spontaneity (2:12). But how do we more immediately let life express itself through us? By way, I believe, of a mystical movement, an extra-cognitive surrender in trust into life itself.

I have already suggested that though Zhuangzi recommends a trustful (and therefore thankful) surrender (or release) into Mystery, the unknowable Totality, the actual 'gate' through which to do so is our most immediate experience of mystery, our self-experience. To entrust oneself to the flow of life is to accept and affirm it within its limits. It is to say Yes to life just as it is given in us. This is not primarily a behavioral expression (acting spontaneously), but an attitudinal orientation from which, presumably, spontaneous activity follows. On the ever present question of how such a mystical movement can be made to happen, I can only admit to ignorance and suggest the only 'method' that these Inner Chapters themselves seem to recommend— imaginative meditation.

Some clarification on my use of the word 'trust' recommends itself here. Trust is essentially an attitude of affirmation—it says Yes to life in its givens. This is an expression of the flow of life itself—to live is to trust. Life is a ceaseless self-affirmation. To trust, therefore, is not to add to the process of life, but rather to follow its flow. I also see trust as in contrast to 'faith'. Faith implies content, something to believe in. But this is to depend on something understood as 'true' where no such assurance is possible. Trust, on the other hand, is so open-ended as to be itself an openness. Nothing need be known or understood, no object or end need be contemplated. It is simple release. This release does not express itself as some form of resignation, a begrudging Okay, but in thankfulness and joy. How do I know? Because life itself manifests as these qualities.

For all his "big words", we are struck with the down-to-earth simplicity of Zhuangzi's valued outcomes. Whereas his proto-Daoist contemporaries of a more religious stripe pursued immortality, union with metaphysical Dao, or realization of rarified *qi* (the 'vital force' of which all things are thought to be composed) Zhuangzi valued that "our bodies will be maintained, our life allowed to flourish, our loved-ones nourished, and our allotted years realized" (3:1). One Confucian contemporary, Xunzi, complained that Zhuangzi was too obsessed with Heaven to understand Humanity, but he clearly had failed to understand him (and that, because he did not wish to do so). What Zhuangzi does is to honestly re-contextualize the human experience into the mystery of its embedding. This negates nothing of the human, but rather seeks to more fully realize its flourishing. True, he has elsewhere followed his advocacy for the outcomes given here with an exclamation that we forget them in favor of "boundlessness" (2:59), but this prioritizing of Heaven is only remedial and still has as its aim human flourishing.

The intended meaning of the reference here to doing good and evil is not entirely clear. It could be, and often is, rendered in the imperative: Don't do so much 'good' as to gain a reputation . . . The greatest 'good' one can do is that which allows its recipients to say, We did it ourselves (*Laozi* 47), and this does not contribute to the building of reputation, a project of becoming 'someone special', and the sage, as we have seen, has no need to be somebody (1:12). Reputation is, nonetheless, often unavoidable as we shall see with the vast tree whose efforts to be completely useless still resulted in a shrine being built beneath it (4:18). The real issue concerns one's intensions. As for not doing *so much* 'evil' as to receive punishment, I think we could take this to mean that in breaking with tradition and convention we should know how far we can go. There's no harm in singing at a friend's wake (6:21), but one would be ill-advised to do so at that of a king. Both reputation and notoriety are also understood as likely to lead to a premature death, and living out "one's allotted years" is an important value within the frame of human flourishing. Still, we understand this value in the context of the aforementioned "boundlessness" where even a premature death is seen as equal to a long life (2:39, 6:10)—nothing can be lost in vastness, however things are arranged.

Another possible understanding of this reference to 'good' and 'evil' is that life, when left to flow without the fetters of a concern about them, will naturally avoid doing too much of either. This could be understood to imply that human nature is inherently 'good', but this would once again import moral discrimination into the mix. It seems more likely that Zhuangzi is saying that life is inherently prone to the realizing of its own flourishing, and this tendency naturally avoids the calculated exercise of 'good' and 'evil'. Here, 'good' is, in fact, the pursuit of reputation; and 'evil' is the pursuit of excessive gain (material or power) which leads to punishment.

HOW TO NOURISH LIFE

The *Zhuangzi* has numerous "skill stories" intended to illustrate the quality and positive results of spontaneous living, but Zhuangzi himself only offers this one of the cook butchering an ox (3:2). This celebrated story is, to my thinking, the best of the lot and offers numerous windows into the workings of spontaneity and the orientation of Daoism generally. We might begin with the choice of a cook to show a king how best to live. Keeping with the important Daoist theme that in a world of ceaseless yang-ing, self- assertion and aggrandizement Dao is best seen in yin, the lowly, scorned, unassuming and unesteemed, Zhuangzi gives us a practitioner of the lowliest of trades, a butchering cook. This is far from incidental, and he uses an entire chapter, the fifth, to make this same point.

"Skill" as used here speaks of intentional doing, the application of knowledge to the task at hand. Following Dao, on the other hand, is allowing things to happen spontaneously, out of the reservoir of one's full life experience, entrusting oneself to "the unthinking parts" of oneself. ("Let your mind spring forth from its rootedness in the unthinking parts of yourself" (23; Ziporyn, p 99). Skill does something; spontaneity provides the opportunity for something to happen. However, the question arises as to whether this could be accomplished without significant cultivated skill, and we see that it could not. The cook had been cutting up oxen for three years before acquiring the necessary skills that enabled his work to find spontaneous expression.

Every way we turn we encounter obstacles, but if we allow things the time and space, they will usually show us a way around them. So it is with the cook, who, rather than angrily hacking at the carcass before him, lets his 'spirit' discover the natural pathways through the ox. His knife seems to have "no thickness" and for this reason, even the tiniest of seams appears as wide and vast allowing the knife plenty of room for "play". The Daoist sage is likewise seen as having "no thickness", being "empty", having no-fixed-self by which to displace or oppose the 'selves' of things and others. Thus, all the world becomes a vast field in which to play and wander. Life lived thus is a "pleasure" to be savored moment by moment.

This, the king realizes, is how best to nourish life. Life is nourished when we allow it to freely up-well and flow through us, unmediated by our calculating minds. Spontaneous living is a consequence of this entrusting of ourselves to the unthinking parts of ourselves. The best way to flow through life is to let life flow through us. Ultimately, the best way to live is not to ask how best to live, but simply to affirm the life in us and to thereby let it live.

THE SINGULARITY OF THE PARTICULAR IN ONENESS

This story of the one-legged Commander-of-the-Right is much more ambiguous than I have rendered it here (3:8). Yet, as rendered I believe it powerfully illustrates two of Zhuangzi's fundamental insights into the workings of language and the implications of his vision of oneness. The interlocutor asks this one-legged man if his one-leggedness is a consequence of birth (Nature) or of the activity of men (either as an accident, war or, more likely, as punishment for some crime). The reply is twofold. First, we are told that everything that happens is Nature. How could it be otherwise? If indeed the Commander lost his leg through the actions of men, how could this still be anything other than the workings of Nature where humanity and everything it does is also just that? Or, are there Two? This holism (some might say with a tone of disapproval, this monism) is inescapable in Zhuangzi. However, this needn't be taken to imply that Nature does the doing (indeed, "Dao does nothing, yet nothing is left undone" (*Laozi* 37)) or that humans do not choose their own doing; it simply acknowledges that whatever happens in the Great Happening *is* the Great Happening, by whatever agency it happens.

The interlocutor is asking after the relationship between Heaven and Humanity, an important consideration for Zhuangzi. He considered it in the metaphor of the forest and its trees where the pipings of earth and humanity were seen as one, in that they are both the piping of Heaven. This is their oneness. Yet, because 'Heaven' simply stands for impenetrable mystery, no 'doer' can be found and we are therefore left to conclude that "each one chooses its own piping" (2:6). This is their not-oneness—and their unassailable uniqueness. He brings this theme up again in the sixth chapter (6:1&7) where we will discuss it further.

The second part of the Commander's reply speaks to the uniqueness of every concrete expression and the inability of language to convey this. His interlocutor wants to understand his one-leggedness by assigning it a category—is it 'this' (Heaven) or 'that' (Humanity), but the Commander refuses to do so and declares it a THIS a la Zhuangzi's declaration of the absolute uniqueness and affirmability of everything by virtue of its simply being. All things are the "uncarved block", the Daoist metaphor for the unknowable Totality, and we use words to chip off pieces so as to make 'sense' of them. This is fine and necessary; but we too easily forget from whence those pieces came. Seeing them again as THIS, rather than as a 'this' or 'that', is returning to a sense of the uncarved block and this is the aim of the Commander's reply.

We can see a similar manifestation of our binary thinking in recent debates about gender-identity. According to the binary mind, one must be either male or female and any sliding of the scale from one side to the other is literally unthinkable. If, however, we can unite them to form a oneness, we can transcend the binary and affirm every expression as THIS, unique, wonderful and affirmable. Similarly, many who are uncomfortable being identified as a binary 'he' or 'she' have chosen THEY. Here we have a very Zhuangzi-like challenge to open our minds to Openness.

EMBRACING THE DANGLE

The concluding story concerning how best to deal with the unavoidability of death foreshadows many others to come. Much of Zhuangzi's philosophy is a consideration of how to reconcile with death, the single most unavoidable event after that of our coming to be at all. He calls this tenuous suspension over the void "the dangle". We can either flee it in denial, fear and mourn it as a catastrophe, or embrace it in thankfulness and acceptance. In the case of the first, this would be to imagine some form of immortality, a common enough practice among the religiously inclined. It is the second, an excessive sense of tragic loss, that Qin Shi finds at the wake for Lao Dan. Since Lao taught the third possibility, thankfully following the natural flow of events, Qin leaves in disgust. Thankfully accepting death, just as one does one's birth, enables one to avoid excessive joy at being born and sorrow at the prospect of death. Joy and sorrow we most certainly and legitimately experience, only these need not depend on the vagaries of fate or be coupled to their opposites. Joy *for* something transforms into sorrow when confronted with the loss of that something. Emotions that *depend on* circumstances disallow free and unfettered wandering. The sage is envisioned as expressing the full range of emotions as spontaneous expressions of her humanity without their affecting her core peace. Thus, her anger is a kind of non-anger, her joy a kind of non-joy, and her sorrow a kind of non-sorrow.

This may be the first extant reference to Lao Dan (Laozi), the legendary author of the *Daodeching* (*Laozi*) and we can't be sure that Zhuangzi did not make him up as he did so many others, though it is equally possible that he simply made use of him as a recognizable legendary figure. It seems likely that this compilation of maxims of 'Daoist' orientation took place around the time of Zhuangzi's writing. Though much of his thought (though not all) is in sympathy with them, he himself makes no reference to them, though they are soon quoted and attributed to Laozi in later contributions to the *Zhuangzi*. In any event, though Zhuangzi identifies him as a sage, he does not give him full marks on his sagacity since his disciples appear to have revered him to the neglect of his teachings. Some translations actually criticize Laozi directly for this failing, while others put the blame solely on the disciples; I have left it ambiguous.

The simple concluding statement (3:12) that though we can see the work of the fire we cannot know where it goes when its work is finished has given rise to a lot of speculation, much of it involving the importation of later philosophical or religious biases (especially Buddhist). Its basic message seems clear enough, however; we observe the workings of life in the animated, but where it goes upon death we have no idea. Nothing more can be said, nor from a Daoist point of view, need be said. Fang Yizhi (1611-1671) so whole-heartedly endorses this not-knowing that he accuses Zhuangzi of faltering in his own commitment to it: "Zhuangzi too makes something of the other side in an attempt to nourish himself on this side, cooking up a pot of Buddha-flesh for his own nutriment" (Ziporyn; p 170). If this were the case, then Zhuangzi would indeed have transgressed his own position. References to becoming something else after one's death—a bug's arm or a rat's liver, for instance (6:17)—might lead one to this conclusion, but, as we have said, Zhuangzi does not understand transformation as guaranteeing a preservation of identity. Nevertheless, he does offer consolation regarding death in his affirmation of death itself as a subsumed in the affirmable Whole. This does not, however, imply any particular outcome. In the end, we are left to affirm or negate the life experience (which includes death), and Zhuangzi chooses to affirm life because it affirms itself.

CHAPTER FOUR
NON-BEING THE CHANGE

THE TEXT (SELECTIONS)—PART ONE

IN THE HUMAN WORLD

1 Confucius' favorite disciple, Yan Hui, came and asked his master for permission to go to the state of Wei. Asked what he would do there, he replied, "The king of Wei has totally mismanaged his state and the people are dying like flies. Now, Master, I have heard you say it is best to leave a well-ordered state for one in chaos since a doctor is most needed where there is the greatest sickness. So, I'd like to go there and formulate some principles derived from your teachings and apply them there. Maybe the state can be saved."

2 "Alas!" answered Confucius, "you'll most likely just get yourself killed! When you are learning a dao, it's best not to complicate it with premature extra-curricular projects; you'll just end up all confused with multiple daos. The great sages of the past, moreover, made sure they had it in themselves before trying to convert others. Since it is not yet fully realized in you, you have no business trying to transform a tyrant. Real sagacity is undermined by a desire for reputation and the cleaver 'application of principles' just results in conflict. Reputation puts others down, and cleverness is only used to win arguments. Neither are the proper tools of the sage. Even if you were beyond these, however, such a tyrant would likely think you were just showing off and trying to make him look bad. This is called 'harassing others', and those who harass others are harassed in return. So, if he is as bad as you say, you'll end up in hot water, and if not so bad, why try to change him at all?"

3 "But let's say you inveigle yourself into court by acting as courtiers do; will you not simply become just like them, or at least have to pretend to be so? Wouldn't this be like fighting fire with fire or draining a swamp by pouring in more water? And in the end, won't the tyrant finally see through your duplicity and leave you dead at his feet? History is full of those who have been of impeccable character, men who rightfully cared for the common man, and yet they met horrible ends. Men of power seek wealth and fame above all else—this is more than the greatest sages can change, much less you. Still, you must have a plan, so let's hear it."

4 "I will be dignified and dispassionate, work hard and stay centered" replied Yan. "Will that work?"

5 "Good grief!" exclaimed Confucius. "Have you heard nothing I've said?"

6 "Well then," replied Yan, "Within, I will be inoffensive and childlike in my honesty while innocently appealing to the words of the ancients as if not offering my own opinions. Though commonly known and accepted, such words have hidden corrective criticisms. Without, I will do as others do, bow and scrape so as to avoid criticism. What do you think?"

7 "I think you might save your skin and accomplish little else," answered Confucius. "The heart of your problem is that you still take your mind as your teacher!"

8 "Well then," replied Yan, "I'm out of ideas. What do you recommend?"

9 "You must fast!" replied Confucius.

10 "My family is very poor," said Yan, "we do lots of fasting!"

11 "That's not the kind of fasting I mean," said Confucius. "I speak of the fasting of the mind. Submerge all your ambitions into one single openness. Then you will hear with not only your ears and your mind, but also with the life force (*qi*) within you. Ears only hear the obvious; the mind hears only what fits its grid; but the life force is an emptiness that allows things to arise of themselves. It is this very emptiness that enables

the view from Dao. And it is the cultivation of this emptiness that is the fasting of the mind."

12 "This I have practiced," replied Yan. "And I found that before doing so I thought I had a concrete identity, but after, I realized that 'I' have never even begun to exist. Is this what you mean by emptiness?"

13 "Exactly!" exclaimed Confucius. "With this you can wander in the tyrant's domain. Where there is an open gate you can enter; where the way is shut, following along with things as they are, it will not concern you. Realizing that all lodgings are one, allow yourself to be lodged in whichever one cannot be avoided. It's easy to leave no footprints when you do not walk, but to walk without touching the ground is hard indeed. Motivated by fixed intentions, it's easy to fake it; but directed by nature, it's easy to be authentic. You know how to fly with wings; now it's time to fly without them. You have learned something of wisdom; now it's time to learn the wisdom of being free of wisdom. Contemplate the emptiness at your very core, and that empty room will fill with light. Success comes when knowing when to stop; not stopping is called 'galloping while sitting'. Turn your senses inward so as to move beyond your calculating mind. Then all things will take shelter in you. This is how things are transformed."

......

THE TEXT—(SELECTIONS)—PART TWO

14 Carpenter Shi and his apprentice were travelling in Qi when they passed by a tree of enormous height and girth and with a shrine beneath it. Though it was surrounded by a throng of admiring tourists, Shi passed it by without giving it a second glance. However, his apprentice could not help but stop and admire it. When he finally caught up with Shi he asked his master why he was not similarly amazed and admiring of the tree.

15 "Enough!" retorted Shi. "This tree is made of worthless wood! A ship made of it would sink, a coffin would rot, a tool would break, a door would leak pitch, and a pillar would be buggy. It's totally useless! Why do you think it lived long enough to get so big?"

16 But when Shi was back home the tree appeared to him in a dream and said, "Why do you insist I be like a domesticated tree? All these are quite 'useful', and for this reason they are plucked, pruned and destroyed. Their usefulness just embitters and shortens their lives. So it is for all things that follow the conventional belief that one's worth is established in one's 'usefulness'. As for me, I've been working hard for countless years to be useless; I have almost failed and tasted the axe, but now I'm entirely useless, and it's a great boon to me. How else could I have become so vast?"

17 "In any case, what business do you, a mere human being about to die, have judging me? Are we not both members of the same class, namely transitory beings? Where in this is there room for pontificating on what is useful and what is not, or whether the one is 'better' than the other?"

18 After Shi awoke, he related this to his apprentice who said, "If it wants to be so useless, why does it have a shrine beneath it?" "Silence!" retorted Shi. "The tree in fact finds it disgraceful to be surrounded by so many admiring sycophants, but it is they who come to it, it does not call them. Still, the shrine itself has helped to keep it from being chopped down. The tree remains, moreover, beyond their conventional values and definitions of one's 'proper' role, and we would do well to do the same."

· · · · · ·

19 Shu the All-Messed-Up was a physical catastrophe. His chin touched his belly, his shoulders were above his head, his ponytail pointed at the sky, his organs were scrambled, and his thigh bones were where his ribs should have been! Yet he easily supported himself by taking in washing and sewing. In addition, when soldiers came to forcefully induct the men, he was passed over. When a work levy was imposed, he was overlooked. However, when it was time to help the disabled, he got three times the allotment. In this way, an 'all-messed-up' body enabled him to live out his allotted years. How much more helpful then might be an 'all-messed-up' 'spirituality'!"

· · · · · ·

20 The forest's trees plunder themselves. The candle burns itself up. The cinnamon tree's bark is edible, so it's ripped off. The lacquer tree's lacquer is useful, so it's lacerated. Everyone knows the usefulness of the useful, but no one seems to realize the usefulness of being useless!

REFLECTIONS—PART ONE

NON-BEING THE CHANGE

The given title for this chapter is "In The World" and its primary concern is how we might best affect positive change in the world. However, since it makes reference to what seems to be some form of meditative practice called "fasting of the heart" (4:11), many commentators focus on this rather than the stated purpose of the chapter and indeed, the purpose of this heart-fasting. This exercise has as its end the discovery of one's inner emptiness, the "empty room" (4:13), and this, in turn will enable one to 'be the change' through non-being the change.

This can be understood as a continuation of Zhuangzi's exhortation that we reconnect with the life within ourselves, the "unthinking parts of ourselves", so as to nourish our individual life experience. This, it turns out, is inseparable from our positive engagement with the world.

Fasting of the mind begins, we are told, with opening ourselves to the reality at our innermost core. This requires putting aside our normal rationalizing, language-bound mind so as to "hear with qi", life itself. When it comes to experiencing life in its immediacy the rational mind can only get in the way since it already has its established interpretive "grid" and can only stand between experience and ourselves in mediation. "Qi" means something akin to "vital force" and has been an important philosophical concept throughout much of Chinese history. Cosmologically, it was widely understood as the fundamental 'stuff' of which everything is composed. Its qualities are not uniform, however; qi settles from its most "quintessential" purity to make denser matter, and for some of Zhuangzi's proto-Daoist contemporaries, the inner cultivation of this most rarefied, quintessential *qi* through meditation was believed to result in a higher state of being. This was essentially a salvific project. Zhuangzi, however, gives it a radically different spin which leads me (at least) to see him as consciously breaking with this tradition—he was as much in contradistinction to what has become the accepted sweep of the "Daoist" tradition as he was to the Confucian. *Qi*, he tells us, is "an emptiness that allows things to arise of themselves." For Zhuangzi, *qi* is not a thing at all, but simply the necessary 'space' in which things can happen. And this emptiness is what we will find at our innermost core. Looking within, we will not find a concrete 'somebody', a soul, but rather, an emptiness that allows the up-welling of life.

Thus, when Yan Hui, Confucius's favorite disciple, practices fasting of the mind he discovers that "'I' have never even begun to exist" (4:12). We have returned to the experience of the sage who has "no-fixed-identity" (1:12) and to Ziqi who lost his 'me' (2:2). And this, for Zhuangzi, is the most important experience we can have: "Just be empty, nothing more" (7:17). Yet, we must 'be' empty only because we fail to realize that we already are. If we were not already empty at our core, then this entire exercise would be bogus—it would be adding to the process of life. Zhuangzi is only suggesting that we come to understand our 'selves' as we really are (and are not). The great thing about this exercise is that we need not look anywhere other than to our own experience, and need not try to become something other than what we already are. Nor should we think this *qi* is anything other than that sense of emptiness that accompanies life as ordinarily and daily experienced. It is always right here, right now, in this very moment, our honest, most immediate and genuine experience—a presence as absence just like the piping of Heaven itself (1:9, 10). Yet if we do not realize this, no cosmic consequences follow—all remains well. Only our immediate enjoyment of life will suffer, and our ability to transform the world will be curtailed.

For we do well to remember the context of this particular presentation of self-cultivation— affecting genuine change in the world. Yan Hui has proposed to change the behavior of a vicious tyrant, and Confucius is instructing him on how to do so without getting killed. His plan as revealed is guaranteed to fail because he wishes to bring his yang to the tyrant's yang; but yang displaces yang, and yang does not appreciate opposition. Yan wishes to "apply principles", bring a program, declare the right way—in a word, he is still yang-ing, taking his mind as his teacher (4:7). Once he has realized his own emptiness, his inner yin, however, then, like *qi*, he can be that emptiness for the tyrant, that space, that occasions transformative change. He will non-be the change.

A common misrepresentation of Zhuangzian 'Daoism' is that it is individualistic and passive—suitable for a hermit. This is simplistic and mistaken. True, Zhuangzi turns philosophic concern from the primacy of the social to the individual, but this never loses sight of the positive social outcomes that the cultivation of one's self entails. Because he is described as having scoffed at offers of political position so that he could continue fishing at the river's edge (17) it is believed he cared nothing for the world. Rather, he simply understood that the world's problems are systemic and that working 'within the system' and using the system's methods cannot therefore solve them. Thus, here we are told: "It's easy to leave no footprints when you do not walk, but to walk without touching the ground is hard indeed" (4:13). The Zhuangzian sage is not a hermit that does not "walk", but one who does so without imposing herself on others. Like Dao, she does nothing yet nothing is left undone (*Laozi* 37).

REFLECTIONS—PART TWO

THE UNITY OF 'MERE BEINGS'

I have not included in my adaptation two lengthy segments that also concern the relation of politics to Zhuangzi's 'Daoism' since they are mostly redundant and add little to what has already been said above. This next story (4:14ff) is also repetitive in that it mostly concerns "the usefulness of the useless" which we have already discussed. I have included it here because it offers a few interesting, if secondary, insights. The first of these is simply Carpenter Shu's attitude of indifference toward this amazing tree. It is useless to his industrial purposes, therefore he does not give it a second look. Where the world is seen as here only *for* the use of humanity we see again the negative consequences of our sense of exceptionalism. Even the preservation of wilderness is represented as a 'resource', a place worthy of preservation only because it provides for human recreation or inspiration. Were it able, all the natural world would no doubt appear to us all in a dream and ask why we, being "mere beings" like everything else, think we have the right to judge the natural world solely on the basis of its "usefulness" to our purposes. Everything has its own self-worth by virtue of its existing at all—this is the message of the tree to Carpenter Shu, and the message of Zhuangzi in his equalizing of all things and our theories about them. Shu has missed the opportunity to participate in the tree's joy and to increase his own in doing so (5:14).

We have already made mention of the unavoidability of reputation, the achievement of a certain 'fame' represented here in the creation of a shrine beneath this tree, for the sage who nonetheless makes no effort to achieve it. There is in Daoist literature a constant tension between these two seemingly contradictory phenomena. She who becomes 'nameless' soon acquires a 'name'. Her emptiness draws others to her as we shall see in the story of the ex-con whose "wordless teaching" attracts more disciples than Confucius, even in his own home state (5:1). Though I have never encountered one, my guess is that we could quickly and easily identify a true sage through her self-emptiness alone. This serves not so much in the identification of a sage, what is likely only a theoretical ideal in any case, but as a means of avoiding attachment to a pseudo-sage, a self-involved 'guru'. We would do better, Zhuangzi tells us, "to evolve along our own daos" (6:8).

ALL-MESSED-UP SPIRITUALITY

The story of Shu the All-Messed-Up (Ziporyn translates "Shu the Discombobulated", p 31) might better fit in the next chapter to which I have given the title immediately above. Shu is a physical wreck, but is still able to not only provide for himself, but for others as well. And not only that, he is able to do so *because* he is all-messed-up. "How much more helpful then might be an 'all-messed-up' 'spirituality'" (4:19)! This strange conception of 'spirituality' is, for me, one of the most powerfully liberating aspects of Zhuangzi's entire vision. We need only return to the

Ziqi's forest to get an idea of how this is so. Each tree has its own unique expression, and whatever that expression, whether healthy or sick, well-formed or broken and twisted, each one is utterly affirmable just as it is. "All-messed-up spirituality" is that 'spirituality' that manifests, not in the enervating self- and world-alienating belief in a hypothetical perfection, but in affirming oneself exactly as one is. It is, as I cannot tire of saying, the realization that we are perfect by virtue of being perfectly who we are. All is well in the Great Mess. This is already and unavoidably as true in us as it is in all things.

This affirmation of what we normally would judge unaffirmable is absolutely crucial to understanding Zhuangzi. When we completely affirm the apparent messiness that is the world we bring all bifurcating judgment to an end and realize that sense of oneness in which all things become THIS and RIGHT. But not only this, we also realize that it is not in *despite* of this messiness that we are able to gain a sense of oneness, but *because of* it. It is only in and through our "not-oneness" that we are able to realize a sense of oneness. Moreover, even this oneness represented in a metaphysical sense, as the "One", is understood as realized through the union of contradictions: "We can call it Tranquility in Turmoil. This Tranquil in Turmoil is complete only as if in turmoil" (6:13).

Ziporyn (p 19) renders a phrase in the second chapter (my 2:54) which I was unfortunately unable to justify in my adaptation but which remains dear to my heart just the same: The sage leaves all things "to their own slippery mush so that every enslavement is also a ennobling." This touches the very heart of Zhuangzi's understanding of 'spirituality'. It is always about making the best possible use of imperfection (the 'useless'), not straining and striving to realize some impossible perfection.

The word that I have here rendered 'spirituality' is *de*, which is usually rendered as 'virtue'. Like *dao*, it is a hugely important word in Daoism and one very difficult to pin down. I understand it most fundamentally to mean the actual, concrete expression of Dao in the world—what a thing is. Everything has its *de*, and in the case of everything except humanity, *de*, like *dao*, cannot be strayed from. Human beings, however, also have *de* as a potentiality, just as they have the realization of psychological Dao as a potentiality (though every expression is Dao and this cannot be lost or gained). Indeed, in the case of human beings, the realization of psychological Dao *is* the realization of their fullest potential, their *de*. In keeping with a more modern expression of this process I have called it 'spirituality'.

CHAPTER FIVE
ALL-MESSED-UP SPRITUALITY

THE TEXT (SELECTIONS)—PART ONE
AUTHENTIC EXPRESSIONS OF DAO

1 In Confucius' home state of Lu there was a man named Wang Tai who had had his foot chopped off for some crime, and yet he had more disciples than the Master himself. Chang Ji wondered at this and spoke with Confucius as follows: "Master, this guy is an ex-con, has no positive teaching and offers no opinions, yet people flock to him empty and leave full. Is there really such a thing as 'wordless teaching', a way of fulfilling the mind without doctrines?"

2 Confucius replied, "This man is a great sage and I, too, take him as my master; only I have been negligent in not going to him. All the world should do so!" "Really?" answered Chang, quite amazed. "What is it that makes him so special?"

3 "Life and death are a matter of great importance to us all, but their relative values do not exist for him at all. Even if the cosmos collapsed, he would not fear being lost with it. Dwelling in non-dependence, he is unmoved by the continual flux. He identifies completely with whatever happens and is thus one with their source."

4 "Seen from the point of view of their differences, even your own organs are as distant as south is from north. But seen from the point of view of their sameness, all things are one. It's just a question of perspective. If you adopt the latter, you no longer rigidly sort things out according to your preferences. You are then able to release your mind to play among all the expressions of Dao. Realizing the unity of all things, you also

realize how nothing can ever be lost. Thus, Wang Tai sees the loss of his foot and the so-called disgrace it was meant to impart as he would the falling of a clod of earth to the ground."

5 "So, he uses his mind to discover its limits and uses the limits of mind to cultivate a mind that is constant in unity with flux," summed up Chang. "But why does this attract so many people to him?"

6 "People cannot see themselves in troubled waters, but only in still water. Seeing themselves in his stillness, they are themselves stilled. All things receive their existence from the same source, but some are able to make better use of it. Like the sage Emperor Shun, Wang Tai is one who is able to help others by not-helping them, this is the value of 'wordless instruction'."

7 "The proof that one has realized this unity is genuine fearlessness. A warrior is considered fearless when he throws himself into battle with abandon; yet this is only because he suppresses his fear for the sake of 'glory'. Genuine fearlessness comes from taking the entire cosmos as one's own body, while seeing one's identity as merely a temporary lodging within it. The sage takes the entirety of her conscious experience and unites it with everything else, and thus has no consciousness to lose. She sees her death as simply one more transformation. So it is with Wang Tai—it is others that seek him out; he feels no compelling need to 'save' them."

· · · · · ·

THE TEXT (SELECTIONS)—PART TWO

8 Toeless Shushan of the state of Lu who had had his foot mutilated as punishment for some crime or another hobbled his way to Confucius to seek instruction. But Confucius treated him rudely and said, "You obviously misbehaved in the past and ended up thus, so isn't it a bit too late to come to me now?"

9 But Toeless retorted, "It's true that I failed to take proper care in the past, but now I have come to you with something much more valuable

than a foot, mutilated or otherwise. Heaven embraces all things and the earth supports them. I thought you, Sir, had realized the Dao of Heaven and earth—it never occurred to me that you would express yourself so!"

10 Confucius was stung, and relented saying, "I was indeed rude; won't you please come in and teach me your dao." But Toeless had heard enough and departed. At this Confucius turned to his disciples and said, "Learn from this, my disciples! Toeless is a mutilated ex-con who still wants to learn; how much more should you who are of much better quality!"

11 As for Toeless, he went to see Lao Dan and said, "Confucius sure is a far cry from being a true sage, isn't he? Why do you think he imitates you so slavishly? He must simply be seeking something as bizarre and delusional as esteem and fame. He clearly doesn't understand that, for the sage, these are cuffs and fetters."

12 Lao Dan replied, "Perhaps you could teach him to see life and death as a single string, and acceptable and unacceptable as a single thread. Might not that perhaps release him from his fetters?"

13 But Toeless answered, "Heaven itself has punished him; how could he ever be released?"

· · · · · ·

14 Confucius said, "Death and life, maintaining and losing, failure and success, poverty and wealth, worthiness and unworthiness, disgrace and esteem, hunger and thirst, cold and heat, all these transpire as a matter of fate. They arise and pass, but we never understand where they come from. Yet still, there is no need to allow them to enter our numinous reservoir so as to disturb our peace. In this way our harmony embraces all experience and unites with their arising so that we are always participating in the springtime of all things. Thus does our mind become the scene of all transformation."

· · · · · ·

15 Huizi asked Zhuangzi, "Can it really be as you say that a human being can transcend his natural inclinations?" "He can," answered Zhuangzi.

16 "But without emotions, how can we call him a human being?" continued Huizi. "Dao gives him his appearance and Nature gives him his form, how could we not then call him a human being?" replied Zhuangzi.

17 Since you call him a human being, then how could he be without natural human inclinations!?" retorted Huizi.

18 "What I mean by natural human inclinations," answered Zhuangzi, "is the constant need to judge some things right and others wrong. What I call transcending them is not allowing our likes and dislikes to enter our hearts so as to disturb our peace, but rather, to follow along with each thing as it is, allowing each 'this' to be This, and thereby adding absolutely nothing to the process of life."

19 "If one does not 'add to the process of life', argued Huizi, "how can one keep his body alive?"

20 "Good grief!" exclaimed Zhuangzi. "Dao gives one an appearance, Nature gives one a physical form, and one does not let his preferences disturb one's peace! But you, on the other hand, treat your own life like a stranger and consume yourself with questions about it instead of actually living it, leaning on your lectern or nodding off at your desk! Nature has given you a life, but instead of learning from it, you end up blabbering about 'hardness and whiteness'!"

REFLECTIONS—PART ONE

DAO IN THE SWAMP

Fortunately, it has become increasingly difficult for most of us to imagine the attitude that the ancient Chinese had toward the disabled. Disability was viewed as a sign of moral failing. Even more so was a disability attributable to corporal punishment at a time when this meant the lopping off of feet, ears and noses. It is our moral duty to keep our bodies "intact" and to have failed to do so is to be a moral disgrace. What better examples could Zhuangzi then use to illustrate his "all-messed-up-spirituality"? For us, characters like Toeless Shushan (5:8) and "Hunchback Limpleg the lipless cripple" (Ziporyn, p 37) are merely humorous, but for Zhuangzi's immediate audience using them as exemplars of 'spirituality' was scandalous. But this use is, in fact, a perfect demonstration of the essence of philosophical Daoism that purposely turns our normative world on its head. The Dao, we are told in the *Laozi*, seeks out those places which are lowest and spurned by humanity—the swamps of the world (8). The reasons for this are at least two, though both are ultimately only provisional and remedial. In this immediate context, Zhuangzi wishes us to realize the unity and equal affirmability of all things just as they are. This again is the message of Ziqi's forest—every tree makes the forest. Where we by default embrace the highest, in also embracing the lowest we return to the unity of all things.

More broadly, where all human self-assertion and self-identification can be seen as a ceaseless yang-ing, Daoism seeks to reconnect us with yin, non-assertion and emptiness. Zhuangzi himself, though he does make mention of yin and yang, makes little use of them in the presentation of his philosophy. I resort to them because they are a wonderfully metaphorical way to illustrate the essential call of Daoism to a re-contextualization with our rootedness in Mystery. They have a long and complex history in Chinese philosophy, however, and in introducing them here many later understandings of them are likely to cloud the waters. The *Laozi* prefers to use Being and Non-Being (1), but these terms too are fraught with misconceptions, chiefly in that they have become metaphysical concepts purporting to represent reality as it 'is'. So, I will stick with yin and yang, and make some necessary qualifications. For our purposes, there is, of course, no yin and yang; they are simply helpful metaphors. Though at some level we might see them as together involved in a ceaselessly cyclic transformation of the one into the other, this is not the primary Daoist use. For Daoism, it is necessary to *prioritize* yin, for the simple reason that humanity as evolved is essentially all about yang-ing. We exist; this is yang. Daoism seeks to re-contextualize our existing with our non-existing (yin). Like the might bird Peng we have arisen from and return to The Pool of Heaven, Mystery. Re-integrating with this reality proves to be the best way to fearlessly and happily do our present existing. Fearfully clinging to yang, our precious 'selves', we experience all the angst and alienation that Zhuangzi earlier described as the bewildering condition of humanity (2:11); uniting our yang with yin—seeing ourselves in the context of, and identifying with the Totality (yin/yang) is freedom to exist without fear in our embedding in non-existence. That's the sum of it. The 'pathetic' characters represented here symbolize this prioritization of yin, the 'lowest'.

A DAO WITHOUT DOCTRINES

In the opening story of this chapter we have such a sweeping overview of Zhuangzi's vision that it's hard to know where to begin. Still, let's begin with 'Confucius'. Zhuangzi's use of Confucius is clearly playful, though never disrespectful. It was a common device in his time and after to use the names of esteemed persons of the past, historical or legendary, to lend weight to one's own teaching, but Zhuangzi never makes any such appeal to authority. His use of Confucius is so blatantly contrary to the actual teaching of Confucius, that his every use of him would have brought a smile to the lips of his intended audience. Zhuangzi is a master of irony, the art of maieutics, midwifery, whereby we are made to engage in the process of birthing our own 'truth'. In his use of Confucius we are required to consider how the words he is made to speak differ from those he actually would have spoken and in that to better understand both and to thereby better judge between them.

Philosophical Daoism is nearly always ironic in that it is perpetually self-effacing. A simple example of irony would be to say in the midst of a rain storm, It's a lovely day! Is it? We think not; but then we might think again that maybe it is. We need the rain. And we can go for a walk later. We are required to engage in a process, to chew our own food. Daoism speaks of Dao, but immediately tells us that this or any spoken Dao is not-Dao. Daoism's action is non-action (*wuwei*). Its knowing is not-knowing. Its anger is not-anger. Its dying is not-dying. Its helping is not-helping. Its being together is not-being-together. And here, its teaching is not-teaching; it is "wordless instruction" (5:1).

Philosophical Daoism is an attempt to present a dao without doctrines, without "positive teachings". Does it succeed? How could it? It can only tell us to take none of what it says as a representation of truth. It's all upayic, all just a finger pointing at the moon—and we all know to look at the moon, not the finger—don't we? If, when we have come to understand Daoism, we are able to believe it without believing it we will have truly understood it. If we in any way whatsoever require that something be true, a "positive teaching", then we will be *dependent* on that which depends on what is undependable; we will have taken our minds as our teacher. Not that the mind is 'bad', not that we should 'pluck it out if it offend' us—rather, we are exhorted to fulfill it. This sage "uses his mind to discover its limits and uses the limits of mind to cultivate a mind that is constant in unity with flux" (5:5). The mind is fulfilled in resting in "the unthinking parts" our experience.

When we identify with the Totality as manifest, as a ceaseless transformation, then our mind becomes 'constant'—constantly transforming without the fear of loss. "Genuine fearlessness comes from taking the entire cosmos as one's own body, while seeing one's identity as merely a temporary lodging within it" (5:7). Again we are challenged to imagine our identity as a "temporary lodging"; to do so is to lose one's 'me', one's objectified and reified subjectivity, one's white-knuckled clinging to a present identity as if fixed and eternal. And this is what enables true "fearlessness", a cardinal quality of sagacity, the realization that in the vastest arrangement any and every arrangement (3+4=4+3) incurs no loss.

Here too we have a clear statement of one of Zhuangzi's most important imaginative exercises: "Seen from the point of view of their differences, even your own organs are as distant as south is from north. But seen from the point of view of their sameness, all things are one. It's just a question of perspective" (5:4). Both the differences and the sameness are 'real'; only because we are chronically absorbed with the former are we enjoined to imagine the latter as a means to realizing a greater sense of wholeness, and this only because it makes for a happier life experience. Seeing all things as one is a way of seeing the world, not a metaphysical statement that declares all things One.

Seeing the sameness of things is an imaginative exercise easily practiced and profoundly effective in giving us a sense of oneness, which in turn frees us from the vexing need to judge between things, deeming some worthy and others unworthy, some affirmable (life) and others as negated (death). When the vast tree (4:17) appears to the carpenter in a dream it is this point of view that it suggests. They are both "mere beings", the same and equal; where then is there room for deeming one more worthy than the other? Rather than dismissing it as useless, therefore, the carpenter could have found his own joy in its flourishing. He could have participated in the tree's own arising, its own "springtime" (5:14).

What cannot be seen as the same as everything else? Yes, even murder and human kindness can be seen as the same. Are they not both human activities? And are not all human activities equally representative of humanity, and that, just as it manifests, an expression of Nature? When this 'road' is realized, the other 'road' of human flourishing can be walked with greater freedom and without allowing the anger that murder arouses to enter our heart and disturb its peace. Anger there is, but it is also a non-anger in that it does not rule us.

This realization of oneness also liberates the mind from its own fixed opinions so as to enjoy all opinions: "You are then able to release your mind to play among all the expressions of Dao" (5:4). Imagine playing among all the world's ideologies as you might among the "contending voices" of the forest's trees, or among the infinitely diverse blooms of its meadow.

Finally, we see here a sage who truly embodies emptiness and thus draws and fills others solely through example, through his silent charisma. His stillness stills others. His not-helping them, helps them. But again, it would be foolish to think that there has ever been such a one, and even more so to seek for such a one today. This, and every Zhuangzian sage, is best seen as an ideal representation of what we can only hope to approximate, while also always remembering that our "every enslavement is also an ennobling."

REFLECTIONS—PART TWO

PUNISHED BY HEAVEN—THANKFULLY

In the next story Toeless Shushan, after a less than satisfactory meeting with Confucius, declares that he (Confucius) has been "punished by Heaven" and is thereby unable to realize the Daoist perspective. Let us rejoice and be glad! For it is not just this most famous and revered of China's philosophers who is so cursed, but probably ourselves as well. So what? Even this final word on our inescapable bondage can be an occasion for freedom and joy where "every enslavement is also an ennobling". And when even failing of this, let that be our ennobling. Yes, this may seem like an infinite regress, but it has its end when we understand how that samsara is Nirvana, delusion is Reality—however much we might try to make it otherwise, all remains well, and ourselves with it. This is not the only occasion when Zhuangzi suggests such an inescapable bondage to the 'normal human inclinations'; in the sixth chapter he has Confucius, in the face of his appreciation of the Daoist ability to "wander outside the boundaries" while he is unable to do so himself, declare to his disciple, "I am punished by Nature. And so probably are you" (6:26). Zhuangzi puts a stake through the heart of all blabber about our supposed spiritual 'birth-right' to become buddhas or whatever 'fully enlightened' beings we might imagine. What a relief! Now we can thankfully be whatever mess we are—and maybe even be transformed thereby.

Toeless has come to Confucius for instruction, but discovers that far from realizing the equality of all things Confucius is completely fettered by judgments of right and wrong, worthiness and unworthiness, dismissing Toeless because of his past 'failures'. Though he tries to make amends, after Toeless has departed he still declares him unworthy compared to his own precious disciples. Toeless then goes to discuss this with Laozi who suggests that he might be cured through envisioning "life and death as a single string, and acceptable and unacceptable as a single thread" (5:12). These imaginative exercises of uniting to form a oneness might liberate him, Laozi suggests. No, Toeless concludes, he is too far gone.

Curiously, Zhuangzi has Toeless say that Confucius slavishly imitates Laozi though only for the sake of reputation, not realizing that the true sage sees fame and esteem as "cuffs and fetters". Later Daoism made polemic use of a legendary story of Confucius coming to Laozi for instruction only to be rebuffed for his ambitions to "be somebody". Perhaps this story was already in circulation at the time of Zhuangzi's writing, or perhaps this story now before us inspired the other.

As for pointing out the "cuffs and fetters" of seeking a name, Fang Yizhi asks: "But do you know what it means to cuff and fetter people with this talk of being released from cuffs and fetters" (Ziporyn; p 182)? Only when we have realized that there are absolutely no conditions that we must meet to be acceptable can we pursue a path of self-cultivation without that too just binding us with more fetters.

PARTICIPATING IN THE SPRINGTIME OF ALL THINGS

I have included a small portion (5:14) of another lengthy story about a Mr. Horsehead Humpback (Ziporyn; p 35ff) whose spirituality matches that of previous examples of sagacity in unexpected packages. In this portion reference is again made to our inner "reservoir", here described as "numinous" though previously described as the Heavenly Reservoir (2:44). I take these as referring to the same phenomenon, namely our experience of being a self-conscious site of an inexplicable up-welling of life. It is self as a continuous open-ended happening, possible only because, like *qi*, it is an emptiness that invites being. It is this that the sage nurtures, and into which she does not allow emotional responses to the endless procession of fated contraries to enter, whether 'positive' or 'negative'. All these things she will experience, and all the emotional responses she will have, but they do not affect her inner peace.

"In this way our harmony embraces all experience and unites with their arising so that we are always participating in the springtime of all things. Thus does our mind become the scene of all transformation." This preservation of one's own inner peace, far from isolating one from the world, unites with it in such a way that can only be described as deeply mystical. Just as we experience ourselves as a joyous up-welling of life, so too do we experience the similar arising of all things. Identified with the endless transformation, we experience ourselves as that transformation. Heady stuff—I wonder if it's possible. It is, in any case, imaginable.

The final story has Zhuangzi in debate with Huizi and further discusses the possibility of transcending the "natural human inclinations" (emotions). As usual Huizi is unnecessarily argumentative and finally an exasperated Zhuangzi tells him he's too occupied with questions about life to actually live it. Questions about 'hardness and whiteness' accompany those about whether a white horse is a horse—how much better to just take *this* horse for a ride, Zhuangzi might say.

It's also instructive to notice that the heart of Huizi's argument entails fixed, language-bound categories. Humans have "natural inclinations" and transcending them would make someone un-human. Zhuangzi, on the other hand, would define humanity as whatever humans might do. Inhumanity is as much humanity as humaneness, though this does not 'excuse' it; life left to flow would not be inhumane, Zhuangzi would contend, though it would take no account of either humanity or inhumanity. We are reminded of the one-legged Commander of the Right's (3:8) response to his interlocutor's desire to have him explain his one-leggedness by putting it in one category or the other, a 'this' or a 'that'. But the Commander replies that it is a "This", that is, a unique, uncategorizable expression of Nature. When we understand the inability of language to appreciate what cannot be said, namely the absolute ungraspable uniqueness of each 'thing', we can also allow words to freely flow between binary poles.

CHAPTER SIX
MY DEATH IS GOOD

THE TEXT (SELECTIONS)—PART ONE

THE GREAT SOURCE AS TEACHER

1 Conventional wisdom tells us: "Understanding what is the doing of Nature and what is the doing of humanity is the ultimate knowledge. What Nature does is bring forth all things. But humanity transcends Nature and takes off on its own. Thus humanity uses what it knows to delve into what it doesn't know about this Source so as to discover how best to live out one's allotted years without being cut off half way." This would indeed be the ultimate knowledge!

2 However, there is a big problem here. And this is that knowledge, in order to be unquestionably 'correct', must depend on something, and that something is strangely unfixed. What humanity 'knows' always and only issues from a subjective perspective, and thus is always accompanied by debate. So, how do I know that what I call Nature is not in fact a fabrication of humanity? How do I know that what I call human activity is not entirely the doing of Nature?

3 There could only be True Knowledge if there were a True Human Being, and I, at least, have yet to meet one. But let us again imagine them in a golden past and see how they would behave:

4 What is a True Human Being? The True Human Beings of ancient times did not rebel against their limitations, had no desire to be fully realized, and saw no need to worry about the future. Thus could they fail without regret and succeed without pride.

. . . . . .

5 The True Human Beings of ancient times knew nothing of loving life or hating death. They arrived without grasping, and left without clinging. They remembered from whence they had come and thus gave no thought to their return. Receiving life, they enjoyed it. Forgetfully, they let it go.

6 This is what it means not to use one's mind to displace Dao. This is what it means to not use one's humanity to imagine a 'better' Nature than Nature. These I would call True Human Beings.

· · · · · ·

7 Thus they appreciated the oneness of things even while appreciating the diversity of things. Their oneness was truly oneness, so that their non-oneness was also oneness. In oneness they followed Nature. In non-oneness they followed humanity. This is what it means for neither Nature nor humanity to displace the other. The one in whom neither Nature nor humanity is displaced, would be a True Human Being.

8 When the pond dries up the fish gather together on the shore so as to spit on each other and keep each other damp. But how much better and how much more natural it is when they can forget all about each other and frolic in the rivers and lakes. So too, instead of praising the sage-emperor Yao and condemning the tyrant Jie, we would do much better to follow and evolve along our own daos.

9 The Great Clod burdens me with a body, has me labor through life, lets me relax in old age, and finally gives me rest in death. Thus, thinking my life good, so also do I think my death good. We might fear the loss of our boat and so hide it in a swamp, but at night a mighty thief might steal it. Hiding the small in the large there is ample room to lose it. But if we hide the world in the world there is no room for anything to be lost. This is the arrangement that guarantees the preservation of all things.

10 Becoming human seems to be simply a matter of chance, but we delight in it just the same. And since the human experience never stops transforming, so also do the opportunities for its enjoyment. And thus the sage uses the human experience to wander in that from which nothing can ever be lost, where all things are preserved. Premature death, long life,

our beginning and our ending, the sage sees them all as equivalent and good. People think they should emulate her, but they'd do much better to emulate that which unites all these transformations, that upon which all things depend.

11 What is this? This metaphysical Dao seems to show itself in the existence of things, but it remains unknowable and unimaginable. We can experience psychological dao in opening up to 'it' as if 'it' were 'there', but 'it' cannot be 'connected with' or experienced as such. For us 'it' is an emptiness. Since it is its own root, it has no dependence on the cosmos, but rather is the source of whatever the cosmos is or contains. It is the highest without being high; it is the profoundest without being deep. It is the oldest without being old.

12 Nanbo Zikui asked Lady Hunchback, "How is it that you are old, yet your face is still like that of a child?" "I have experienced Dao," she answered. "Can I also experience it?" he asked. "No way!" she replied. "You don't have what it takes."

. . . . . .

13 "The One is that which sends all beings out and receives them back again. It destroys all and generates all. We can call it Tranquility in Turmoil. This Tranquil in Turmoil is complete only as if in turmoil."

. . . . . .

THE TEXT (SELECTIONS)—PART TWO

14 Ziji, Ziyu, Zili, and Zilai fell into conversation together. They concluded that, "Whoever can take his head for nothingness, his spine for life, and his ass for death, whoever understands that life and death, existence and non-existence, are a single body—that one will be our friend!" At this they laughed and bonded together as friends.

15 Not long afterwards, Ziyu became deathly ill and Ziji went to see him. Ziyu, whose body had become terribly contorted, exclaimed, "How great is the Creator of Things that has made me thus!" For though he was a

physical mess, still his mind was at peace. After dragging himself to the well to see his reflection, he again exclaimed, "The Creator of Things has sure messed me up!"

16 "Doesn't this bother you?" asked Ziji. "Not at all," replied Ziyu, "what's there to be bothered about? Who knows what the next transformation will bring!? Will my left arm become a rooster to announce the dawn, or my right arm a crossbow bolt to put an owl on the table, or my ass wheels and my spirit a horse and chariot to ride in? In any case, life comes when it comes and leaves when it leaves; it's just a matter of contentedly following along with wherever one is in the process, and not allowing dependent joy or sorrow to enter one's mind. This is what the ancients called "the dangle and release". Though we cannot avoid either, we can release ourselves from worrying overmuch about both. This is why I say, 'What's to be bothered about?'"

17 Soon after, Zilai got sick! Zili went to see him and found him gasping on his deathbed and surrounded by his weeping family. "Hush!" he shouted, "don't disturb him at his time of transformation!" Then, to Zilai he said, "How great is Transformation-Creation! What will become of you? Where will you go? Maybe you'll become a rat's liver or a bug's arm."

18 Zilai replied, "A child must obey his parents and go where he is told, how much more should one obey the direction of yin and yang. The Great Clod burdens me with a body, has me labor through life, lets me relax in old age, and finally gives me rest in death. Thus, thinking my life good, so also do I think my death good."

19 "What if a master blacksmith were working some metal and it leapt up and said, 'I insist you make me a mythical sword!'; surely this would be an inauspicious lump of metal! Similarly, if because I was blessed to have been a human I now insisted on being the same again, surely I would be an inauspicious lump of person. Viewing Transformation-Creation as a master blacksmith, and heaven and earth as its vast furnace, what could I become that would not be good? Suddenly I sleep. Suddenly 'I' awake."

20 Zisanghu, Mengzifan, and Ziqinzhang happened to meet each other and said, "Who can be together yet not be together, help each other by not helping each other? Who can ascend to the heavens, wander in the mists, rambling without restraint, living in mutual forgetfulness without end?" At this they looked at each other and burst out laughing in complete agreement and became fast friends. But at that very moment, Zisanghu fell down dead.

21 Confucius, hearing of this, sent his disciple Zigong to the wake. There he found the two remaining friends, composing a song and playing the zither, and then singing a silly ditty: "Hey Sanghu, hey Sanghu, Will you return? No, you've gone to what we essentially are, leaving us still human!" Completely outraged, Zigong exclaimed, "Is this the proper ritual for seeing off the dead!" But the two just laughed and said, "What does this fellow know about the real purpose of ritual?"

22 When he had returned to Confucius, Zigong related this incident and asked, "What kind of people are these who don't bother to cultivate their persons, treat the body with disregard, and sing to a corpse!?"

23 Confucius answered, "These are men who wander outside the boundaries, while I must wander within them. These two paths do not meet. It was silly of me to have sent you."

· · · · · ·

24 "Carefree they wander beyond the dust and dirt, free and unfettered in the doing of nothing in particular. Why would they bother with conventional ritual just to please others?"

25 "But Master, then why have you chosen the path you follow?" asked Zigong.

26 "As for me," answered Confucius, "I am punished by Nature. And so probably are you."

· · · · · ·

27 Yan Hui came to Confucius and asked about a certain man praised for his skill at mourning, though he was clearly devoid of any deep grief. "Even when his mother died Mengsun Cai wailed but shed no tears, and even though he was not sorrowful in the depths of his heart, he became renown as an exemplary mourner throughout the state of Lu. How can you explain this?"

28 "Mengsun has truly understood death in understanding the implications of not understanding it," answered Confucius. "When you attempt to clarify things and find that they cannot be clarified, they will nevertheless clarify themselves if allowed to do so. He understands nothing of why we live or die, from whence we arrive or to whence we go. Thus, having transformed into a human being, he simply awaits the next unknowable transformation without fuss. He understands that, when transforming, he can know nothing of not-transforming, and when not-transforming, he can no know nothing of transforming—what can he know of the 'before' and 'after'?

29 "You and I who take death as an immitigable loss have not yet awakened to this reality. He, on the other hand, remains unharmed by the thought of death. Since life is for him but a momentary lodging, he does not see life as something he can lose, and thus does no real 'dying'. Thus, he alone is awakened. He mourns only because others do, and he simply accommodates himself to their needs."

30 "We inexplicably discover ourselves involved in the experience of being human and then assign ourselves a concrete identity and call it 'myself'. But how do we know that this self-identity has any reality to it? If you dream you are a bird, you think yourself a bird-identity and fly; if you dream you are a fish, you think yourself a fish-identity and swim. Might not I now be dreaming I'm a human-identity and thus do the human thing? When we laugh, it is spontaneous and not because we have carefully reasoned things out; so too with being human."

31 "When you understand your present 'identity' in the context of the ever-transforming, no matter what that present 'identity' might be, and

yet fully embrace it and play within it as a unique and distinct expression, then you experience the obvious oneness of Nature."

32 Yierzi left the presence of Yao and came to Xu You who asked, "What did you learn from Yao?" Yierzi replied, "He taught me to pursue humanity and responsibility, and to make clear the difference between right and wrong."

33 "Good grief!" exclaimed Xu You. "Why did you come to me? Yao has already tattooed your face with humanity and responsibility and de-nosed you with right and wrong! How could you ever wander free in the untrodden wilds?"

34 "Sill, can I not wander along its borders?" pleaded Yierzi.

35 "Impossible," replied Xu You.

. . . . . .

36 "But how do you know the Creator of Things won't erase my tattoo and restore my nose?" Yierzi persisted. "Ah, it is indeed unknowable!" Xu You replied.

. . . . . .

          . . . . . .

37 Yan Hui came to Confucius and said, "I've made progress." "How so?" asked Confucius. "I've forgotten humanity and responsibility," answered Yan. "That's great, but you've still got some way to go," said Confucius.

38 Sometime later Yan again came and said, "I've made progress." "How so?" asked Confucius. "I've forgotten ritual and music." "That's great, but you've still got some way to go."

39 Sometime later Yan came once again and said, "I've made progress." "How so?" asked Confucius. "I just sit and forget," answered Yan. Shocked, Confucius asked, "What do you mean?" "I forget my physical

self, lose my physical senses, leave my mind behind and become the same as the Transforming Openness."

40 "The same!?" exclaimed Confucius. "Then you're beyond preferences! Then you are yourself a transforming and have no fixed constants! You are truly the worthy one. Please, I beg to be your disciple!"

......

REFLECTIONS—PART ONE

MY DEATH IS GOOD

Some commentators have suggested that the "Great Source" referenced in the title to this chapter is death itself. This, in my view, is stretching things a bit though, from a certain point of view, *everything* we encounter is that Source, and among these death is perhaps the most uncompromisingly pressing. The chapter does, however, take several brief descriptive forays into the realm of metaphysical Dao (6:9, 13, 15, 19), and we can take these as inspiring the chapter's title. Still, death looms large both in life and as the subject here. It is, for Zhuangzi, the single most important event in the "procession of fate" that impacts our enjoyment of life, and for this reason the one to which he devotes a significant part of his attention.

We are invited here to understand how it can be said that if life is good, then so also is death (6:9). The proof that one has done so consists in one's ability to truly believe: *My* death is good. Could there be a more simple, yet difficult, nut to crack? Imagining how this might be so, and how it would feel in me to fully embrace it, is an exercise that promises a reward commensurate with its difficulty, however.

NOT-ONE IS ALSO ONE

The chapter opens with a provisional statement reminiscent of that which opens the third chapter, a consideration of the apparent contrast between the activities of Nature and those of humanity— where does the one end and the other begin? This morsel of conventional wisdom reflects a long thread of philosophical thought and methodology in which it is thought that if we can just figure out the "principles" by which Heaven operates, then we can use these to guide our life and society to their best possible conclusions. Zhuangzi, of course, will have none of it. It is in the first place unlikely that we could know these principles, and if we did, to know that we know them. Secondly, to *apply* our supposed knowledge to life would be to add to the process of life, making it conform to an idea, and this would alienate us from life itself by way of a mediating mind.

During a hypothetical excursion into a golden past inhabited by "true human beings", Zhuangzi finally ties up his own thoughts on this issue: "Thus they appreciated the oneness of things even while appreciating the diversity of things. Their oneness was truly oneness, so that their non-oneness was also oneness. In oneness they followed Nature. In non-oneness they followed humanity. This is what it means for neither Nature nor humanity to displace the other. The one in whom neither Nature nor humanity is displaced, would be a True Human Being" (6:7). This is, in effect, walking two roads simultaneously—appreciating the unity of all things as Nature, on the one hand, and the manyness of things consequent to the inherent dualism of human self-consciousness, on the other. Not-oneness is also oneness, though not to the loss of its not-oneness. This works out practically thusly: Though Nature is understood as amoral, we can still appreciate the need for human moral distinctions; though language can only artificially chip off parts from the uncarved block, still we can use it to approximate understanding; though the rational mind has its limits, still we can use it to our benefit within those limits; though "all is (ultimately) well", we can still work to improve things; though Nature is indifferent, we can still care; though joy and sorrow, contentment and anger that depend on circumstances need not disturb our inner peace, still we can experience them. It's really all very simple, if paradoxical.

The idea that Nature could yield True Knowledge so that its principles could guide human activity would require a True Human Being, a fully realized sage, and Zhuangzi sees this as beyond even a hypothetical possibility. Still, there's value in imaging such a one.

I have included only those attributes that seem to best demonstrate Zhuangzi's message. They "did not rebel against their limitations, had no desire to be fully realized, and saw no need to worry about the future. Thus could they fail without regret and succeed without pride" (6:4). They could affirm themselves just as they were and thus could proceed in their self-cultivation without alienation from their present. They enjoyed life, but saw no reason to cling to it (6:5). And, importantly, they did not anthropomorphize Nature—did not make it moral, rational or purpose driven (6:6). In a word, they did not interpret the world religiously.

HIDING THE WORLD IN THE WORLD

As if inspired by his description of the ancients Zhuangzi next segues into a succession of vivid metaphors that wonderfully express his own philosophy. First, we have the fish that, when in distress, go to extremes to facilitate mutual support (6:8). This is great, but it is not the way fish would normally choose to live. It is rather their nature to freely frolic in the rivers and lakes (a Zhuangzian metaphor for the realm of freedom in non-dependence), forgetting all about each other. We expect that for many this vision of the ideal human as forgetting all about others in their non-dependence might seem more an expression of inhumanity, than of humanity at its best. Yet, later in the chapter we have three friends make precisely this the foundation for their friendship: "Who can be together yet not be together, help each other by not helping each other? Who can ascend to the heavens, wander in the mists, rambling without restraint, living in mutual forgetfulness without end" (6:20)? If non-dependence is a way to live in freedom then that way which best facilitates it in oneself and in others is this mutual forgetfulness—things flourish when left to naturally arise from within themselves. But it is still a being together without being together and a helping of one another without helping one another. In other words, it is not indifference to the well-being of others, but rather a genuine caring that knows the effectiveness of *wuwei* and emptiness in bringing that well-being about for others as well as for oneself.

Zhuangzi's Confucian contemporary, Mencius (ca. 372-289 B.C.E.), relates the story of an old "man from Song" (the butt of many an early ethnic joke and twice used by Zhuangzi (1:13, 20)) who wanted to help his son's rice to grow and so, by the light of the moon, pulled each plant up a little higher. In the morning, the son discovered all his plants were dead. People, like rice, are best helped when given the opportunity to natural grow of themselves.

Zhuangzi also pointedly says here that dependence on others is especially to be avoided when it comes to deciding how best to live. Whether focused on an august sage or a great villain, these are equally a distraction where one's dao is best left to arise from one's on life experience.

Next, Zhuangzi introduces his celebrated suggestion that we "hide the world in the world" (6:9). If we hide something small in something big, there is always ample room to lose it. If, on the other hand, we identify with the Totality, where is there room for 'us' to get lost? If we take our identity as fixed, this is a very small thing indeed, and something separated from everything else. If like Ziqi, however, we so identify with Nature that our insular 'me' falls away, where in Nature can 'we' be lost? We are Nature. We can hide the 'world' in the world when we realize ourselves as that 'world'. All this is facilitated by uniting opposites to form a oneness. Ziqi united self and other—not just some one 'other', but every other—he became the world. Laozi suggested above, that we see life and death as a single thread and acceptability and unacceptability as a single string, that is, make them one. These psychological movements in themselves facilitate becoming the world. Indeed, any one similar movement ineluctably opens into the uniting of all things.

Zhuangzi also here again speaks of the Totality as an "arrangement" of the manyness of things; this psychological sense of Oneness does not negate our experience of not-oneness. It is as we saw with the monkey trainer (2:26) who understood that however the distribution of nuts was arranged, whether 3+4 or 4+3, no loss would or could be incurred.

Reference here to the 'source' as The Great Clod is wonderfully and significantly irreverent. It gets tiresomely trite, let's face it, speaking of the Great Unknowable Mystery/Dao/Source. Zhuangzi here provides us with a bit of humorous relief. Given his conclusions in the second chapter, he might just as well have called it The Great Horse. We do well to keep this in mind when shortly we read of "The Creator of Things" (6:15). It is important also to remember that Zhuangzi was not theo-phobic since neither he nor his culture had ever committed itself to a fixed and uncompromising theism. By contrast, I, having previously been a theist, experience some discomfort with such references.

Finally, we have here that statement from which I have taken the title for this chapter: "Thus, thinking my life good, so also do I think my death good." I can think of no other more powerful expression of the shout of thankful affirmation that Zhuangzi's philosophy evokes. Why Yes! and not No!? 'Because' life itself says Yes. Only the rationalizing and discriminating mind could conjure up a No. We "delight" in life, Zhuangzi tells us (6:10), even though our experience of it seems purely accidental. And since life itself is a continuous process of similar accidental circumstances, the sage sees them all as further opportunities for enjoyment. Such is the value of understanding the equality of all things.

But once again Zhuangzi warns us against taking a sage as our teacher, something that would mediate between ourselves and our own most immediate experience. We need not take this as abjuring all teachers, but as a precautionary note should we find one. What we can emulate, and even *depend on,* is that upon which everything depends (6:11)—the unknowable and ungraspable—the "Transforming Openness" (6:38). But, as we have seen, this is tantamount to depending on nothing in particular.

Because of their importance to the Zhuangzi's overall message I have included two snippets of a story about Lady Hunchback's response to an aspiring sage. What I have edited out is a lengthy description of stages supposedly leading to 'enlightenment'. In this, my bias is clearly manifest. Some commentators of a more literalistic—I would say 'religious'—bent make much of this description and I would refer the reader to them should they have a similar interest. What interests me in the first snippet is her unambiguous pronouncement that this would-be sage does not have the makings of a sage (6:12). Period. As with the discovery of Confucius' similar "punishment", this is as liberating as its contrary—perhaps more so. Need I say why?

The second snippet (6:13) contains Lady Hunchback's description of the Totality as "Tranquility in Turmoil", which as we have previously discussed, invites us to discover our own tranquility in the midst of and *through* our turmoil. And this serves to answer the question above.

REFLECTIONS—PART TWO

WHAT'S TO BE BOTHERED ABOUT?

What follows are three delightful stories that wonderfully illustrate Zhuangzi's suggested attitude toward death and dying. Since I have already dipped into them in several previous discussions, and since they are largely self-explanatory, I will mostly leave them to speak for themselves. The essential message is that our fear of death can be largely overcome when we unite life and death into a single body (6:14)—life and death naturally arise together, and it seems natural enough that we should accept them as a single package, as "a single string" (5:12). Our fear and distaste for death, far from being 'natural', is precisely the opposite. Zhuangzi invites us, as always, to imagine our experience of being human in the largest possible context. Thus, in loving and affirming life, it naturally follows that we should also love and affirm death. This is the affirmation of all things, Zhuangzi's joyful and thankful Yes! Since Zhuangzi's philosophy of life is really simply about learning to enjoy life to the fullest, and not to realize some escapist experience that negates how it actually manifests, we can say that this particular psychological movement of uniting our life and our death in thankfulness is at the very heart of his purpose.

WANDERING ALONG THE BORDERS

Next (6:32), we are re-introduced to Yao, a patron saint of the Confucians, and Xu You, the sage who previously rejected Yao's offer of the Empire (1:13). A disciple of Yao, Yierzi, comes to Xu You for instruction, but has been so tainted by the 'positive teachings' of right and wrong and the two cardinal Confucian virtues of benevolence and righteousness, that Xu tells him he is beyond help. What could possibly be wrong with benevolence and righteousness? Nothing, if they arise naturally; much if they are imposed from without.

Having been told that he could not possibly "wander free in the untrodden wilds" Yierzi asks if he might then possibly wander along its borders? "Impossible!" is the emphatic reply. This echoes Confucius' realization that he is "punished by Nature" in that he cannot wander "outside the lines" of convention as does the Daoist sage. But Yierzi persists and Xu You admits that it may be possible after all and thus proceeds to describe his dao (which I have omitted). This, to my thinking, opens up to the idea of approximation. It may very well be the case that all these "big words" are impossible to realize, that no one could ever fully embody this vision. If this troubles us, then something is amiss; we may have taken metaphor for reality or even worse, fallen into the trap of believing that there are conditions that we must meet to be fully affirmable. Between Yierzi and Xu You there is no difference; they are equally affirmable, perfect by virtue of being perfectly who they are.

Still, these "big words" are saying something even after being understood as saying nothing 'true'. A dao does open up before us—a path that suggests the possibility of approximatingly realizing what in the end can only be an idealist dream. We might still be able to wander along the borders of this vision, enjoying the view of those distant 'wilds', and perhaps even transform the borders themselves into our own unique 'wilds'. This vision is, after all, always about right now, just as we are. We wander where we are, not where we are not.

THE JOYS OF FORGETFULNESS

The concluding story of this chapter that I have chosen to include has Yan Hui reporting his incremental "progress" in forgetfulness to Confucius until he "just sits and forgets" (6:37). This enables Yan to be "the same as the Transforming Openness". Confucius, the indisputable Master, understands this as the ultimate mystical experience and begs to be Yan's disciple. Despite the serious ideas embedded here, clearly Zhuangzi also wishes to make us laugh. His ironic iconoclasm reaches its zenith here. The serious intent of the story is, however, also directly proportional to the extent of its humor. With Zhuangzi, the funnier something is, or the more bizarre, the more important its messages are likely to be.

The first of these messages is the one suggested in the previous story, namely that the Confucian project of moral self-cultivation is counter-productive in that it "adds to the process of life". If the Confucian virtues of benevolence and righteousness (the fulfilment of one's social duties) are innate to humanity, then from the Daoist point of view they will manifest themselves when life itself is allowed to express itself. Otherwise, we need not concern ourselves with them. This is a sticky point for both schools. Confucius took his guidance from the past, the imagined moral conventions of the then defunct Zhou dynasty. That's why "ritual and music" were taken to be important methodological components of self-cultivation. We are required to *conform* to pre-existing norms. Mencius, though remaining a committed Confucian, was aware of the need to discover a foundation for moral behavior beyond conventional and, frankly, culturally relative precedent. He found it in the innate nature of humanity; human beings are essentially moral beings, though unfortunately largely estranged from their own moral conscience. His project of self-cultivation thus takes on its own mystical dimension wherein one nurtures this inner reality. The Confucian Xunzi (fl. 298-238 B.C.E.) took the opposite tack; humanity is essentially immoral and requires external controls, a "straightening board", to be made moral. My sense is that Zhuangzi saw the question as moot; to concern oneself with moral outcomes is to already be fettered by questions of right and wrong. Still, we do not see a Zhuangzian sage acting in any way immorally, though some might take issue with her apparent indifference. In any event, we do see in Zhuangzi's call to the affirmation of all things what amounts to the heart of Confucius' moral doctrine of *shu*, "likening to oneself". This equates to Confucius' negative expression of the Golden Rule: Do not do to others what you do not want done to you (*Analects* XII, 2). Zhuangzi's vision of complete pan-affirmation paves the way for such behavior, though to say so would be to cut it off at its root. He is not a moralist.

Yan's experience of being "the same as the Transforming Openness" is, of course, the heart of the story. He has so identified with the mystery of apparent reality that the qualities of non-discrimination and openness have become his own. He, too, is happily unfixed and contentless. Openness is that quality that arises from being of unfixed-identity and exercising unfixed-knowing. All things can be equally embraced because no one thing is embraced at the exclusion of others. Mystery is not a 'thing', but an emptiness—the lack of anything fixed and sure.

The question arises once again if Zhuangzi is here advocating for some form of meditation. It certainly seems so on the surface, but I am not so sure. In my view, his proposed outcome of being "the same as the Transforming Oneness" is itself presented as fantastic and hyperbolic rather than as a fixed and realizable goal, and this puts the method of its 'realization' in a similarly metaphorical light. Nevertheless, the use of meditative methods might be helpful in the approximation of Zhuangzi's mystical vision, if not pursued with the view of attaining some imagined fixed metaphysical goal. This, to my thinking, would be to negate what is Zhuangzi's most fundamental point of departure—the eschewal of all 'positive teachings'.

Finally, we have all this "forgetting". Suggestions that we forget one thing or another are so common in Zhuangzi that it clearly plays an important role in his philosophy. The classic expression of what is implied by forgetting appears in a skill story in the 19th chapter of the *Zhuangzi*: "The forgetting of the foot means the shoe fits comfortably. The forgetting of the waist means the belt fits comfortably. And when the understanding forgets right and wrong the mind fits comfortably. When the encounter with each thing fits comfortably the internal is not altered and the external is not made master. When everything fits, from beginning to end, even this fitting is forgotten, and that is the perfect fit" (Ziporyn; p. 82). Here, forgetting simply refers to that state of spontaneous being where things don't bother us. It is not wrestling with them so as to keep them from "entering our numinous reservoir", but having no need to think about them at all. Thus Yan, when he "just sits and forgets" (6:39), has reached a point in which nothing concerns him—not even—especially not even—whether he is "the same as the Transforming Openness" or not. The "perfect fit" is when even fitting is forgotten; when one's becoming proceeds without worrying about the need to achieve anything. It is simply being comfortable with who one is. Or are we meant to strive to be comfortable, and therefore never actually be comfortable?

It is also worth noting that the greatest stated value here is being comfortable—not 'good', not 'useful', not 'successful', not 'esteemed', not 'remembered'—just comfortable. And this I would describe as a carefree happiness that does not depend on circumstances.

We forget ourselves by letting ourselves grow in continual self-affirmation. We forget our friends and the world by not imposing ourselves upon them, but rather by being the inviting space for them to grow and transform of themselves. This again is non-being the change. We have forgotten our dao when it arises as a matter of course, not as something applied. It is then that Dao is not-a-dao.

CHAPTER SEVEN
IT'S JUST BEING EMPTY

THE TEXT (SELECTIONS)—PART ONE

KINGLY WORDS FOR RULERS

1 Four times Nie Que asked Wang Ni about what he knew and every time he answered, "I don't know." This elated Nie Que so much that he went and related it to Puyizi who replied, "Finally you get it! For this reason I say the clan of Emperor Shun is no match for the rulers of the Tai clan. The rulers of the Shun family still think they know what humaneness is and impose it upon others. Most of their subjects think this is fine, but consequentially neither the rulers nor the people can stop treating others inhumanely. A ruler from the Tai clan, on the other hand, sleeps like a rock and awakes without a care. Sometimes he thinks he's a horse, other times he thinks he's an ox—he has no-fixed-identity and thus sees no need to impose himself upon others. This is the greatest 'knowledge' and a true expression of Dao. For these never lead him to disparage others or to treat them inhumanely."

· · · · · ·

2 Heavenly Root was wandering on the south side of Abundance Mountain when he came upon Man-With-No-Name on the bank of Calm River. "Can you tell me how best to rule the world?" he asked.

3 "Bugger off, you fool!" Nameless shouted. "What a stupid question! I was just about to go hang out with the Creator of Things, and when I tired of that, to mount a bird of mist and fly off beyond the knowable world, to the land of nothing in particular, the vast and borderless wilds. Why have you come here to bother me with stupid questions about ruling the world!?"

4 But Heavenly Root was undeterred and asked again. Man-With-No-Name relented and said, "Let your mind wander in the indeterminate, unite your heart with the silent vastness, affirm the rightness of each thing as an expression of Nature without imposing your own biases—then the world will be well governed!"

5 Yang Ziju came to Lao Dan with a question about what makes for a good ruler. "I know a man who is quick-witted, a fast-riser, and brilliant—a real 'winner' who diligently studies Dao. Might he be compared to the sage-kings of old?"

6 "Compared to the sage-kings of old," replied Lao Dan, "he is only material enough to make a petty bureaucrat or a fortune-teller who believes his own nonsense, someone who harms his own body and vexes his own mind. It's because of the beauty of leopards and tigers that they lose their skins. The antics of a monkey and the rat-catching skills of a dog put them on the leash. Could these be favorably compared to the enlightened kings?"

7 Completely taken aback, Yang asked, "Tell me, please, how then does an enlightened king rule?"

8 "When an enlightened king rules," Lao Dan replied, "his positive influence covers the entire world, but no one knows it comes from him. He transforms the world, yet no one depends on him. He remains unnamed, thus all the people are able to delight in themselves. He dwells in the unknowable and wanders where nothing in particular exists."

THE TEXT (SELECTIONS)—PART TWO

9 There was a powerful shaman named Zheng who could predict people's death and the twists and turns of their fortunes with incredible accuracy. When people saw him, they wisely turned and ran. But Liezi sought him out and when he heard his fortune he was completely taken in by and enamored of him. Thus, returning to Huzi, his own teacher, he declared,

"I used to think your dao was the ultimate, but now I have found a dao that far exceeds it!"

10 Huzi replied, "I have only shown you the mere outlines of this dao, yet you think you've mastered it? You're like hens that yearn for chicks, yet have no rooster. For you, a dao is a path to power with which you wish to dominate others, insisting that they adopt your views. This is precisely why this shaman could so easily dominate you. He easily read your ambitions on your face. Bring him here and let him give my face a go."

11 So, the next day Liezi brought the shaman who after encountering Huzi exclaimed, "Your master is on the verge of death! He's as if already dead! All I saw was wet ashes!"

12 Weeping copiously, Liezi returned to his master to tell him the bad news. "I only showed him the patterns of the earth, still in chaos before the mind sets them in 'order'. He probably sensed my existence still unformed and unknowable. Bring him again."

13 The next day the shaman was back and declared to Liezi, "Your master is greatly improved. How fortunate he is to have met me! His inner constipation is again moving!"

14 When Liezi reported this to Huzi the latter said, "This time I showed him *heaven's* patterns. Beyond articulation, beyond words and identities, beyond all plans, yet it is still experienced as the promise of existential flourishing. Bring him again."

15 This time the shaman told Liezi, "Your master is chaotic; I cannot read his face. Give it a few days, maybe he'll settle down."

16 "This time I showed him a great flourishing gushing forth without individuation. Why not bring him again?"

17 The following day the shaman took one look at Huzi and fled in fear. "Try and catch him!" Huzi exclaimed, but he was already too far down the road. "This time I showed him 'me' before I am 'me'—just an empty,

chaotic impulse with no identifiable who or what. That's why he ran away."

18 At this Liezi finally realized that when it comes to Dao, he was clueless. So he returned home where he remained for three years, forgetting all convention—cooking for his wife and treating his pigs like honored guests—abandoning all 'spiritual' ambition, and allowing his carefully carved character to return to the uncarved block. Like a clod of earth, seemingly a chaos, he thus remained for the rest of his days.

. . . . . .

. . . . . .

19 Thoroughly embody endlessness and wander where nothing has yet to begin. Thoroughly realize the experience that Nature allows, but don't think you've gained anything thereby. Just be empty, nothing more.

20 The fully realized person is like a mirror; it reflects all things, while not rejecting, welcoming, or storing them. In this way she can respond to all things and events without harm.

21 The emperors of the Southern and Northern Seas frequently met in the land of the Middle whose emperor was Chaos. Thinking to repay him for his hospitality they decided to give him the seven holes of humanity which he presently did not have. So, every day they gave him a new hole. On the seventh day, Chaos died.

REFLECTIONS—PART ONE

HOW BEST TO GOVERN

Though snippets of wisdom concerning how best to govern are sprinkled throughout the Inner Chapters, those stories most directly addressing this concern have been assembled here. Since few of us are likely to become emperors, kings, or even executives, and since those who actually are, are unlikely to take any of this wisdom to heart, we must seek to understand how it is applicable to our own more mundane lives. But this is not really all that difficult given that we are all the 'rulers' of ourselves and daily encounter situations which require 'political' acumen. The essential Daoist lean toward yin, allowing things the space to become, moreover, is equally applicable to every aspect of life, social and political, as well as personal. This 'lean' is internalized in the realization of no-fixed-identity, as metaphorically illustrated by the ruler who sometimes thinks he's a horse, and other times thinks he's an ox (7:1).

In the first vignette we see how our understanding of our not-knowing leads to an acknowledgment that we are not in a position to definitively declare what is 'best' for anyone, and this, in turn, dissuades us from imposing our views on others. There are many, of course, who prefer being so directed, but this is ultimately counter-productive. In the case of 'humaneness', 'knowing' and imposing what is considered humane ends up being inhumane, and those who take these definitions onboard themselves become inhumane. The reason for this is simple enough; where humanity is defined and imposed it remains exterior to a person's inner life. As such, it is a thing to be used, not a way to actually be.

In the second vignette a reluctant hermit sage is pressed to explain how best to govern: "Let your mind wander in the indeterminate, unite your heart with the silent vastness, affirm the rightness of each thing as an expression of Nature without imposing your own biases—then the world will be well governed" (7:4)! This is likely not what the interlocutor expected to hear, nor what we would expect politicians to take onboard given that politicians, by definition, are those who wish to rule over others.

It's easy to read these words without stopping to explore the possibility of their proximal realization; we've already read similar words so many times before. Yet, though we would probably do well to not take them too seriously, that is, literally, still Zhuangzi offers them with something more than the spinning of fantasies in mind. At minimum, he likely wished that we would attempt to imaginatively 'try them on'. All three suggestions offer very real opportunities for imaginative envisioning. "Let your mind wander in the indeterminate." If wandering is a kind of unattached freedom of movement, then it clearly cannot cling to any one dao. But if this is the case, then this dao on offer here must also be "forgotten". "When everything fits, from beginning to end, even this fitting is forgotten, and that is the perfect fit (19)." Zhuangzi's dao is one that enables freedom to wander in the harmony of every expression (*de*) (5:4). Yet, to accomplish this, that dao must understand how that it, too, is just another dao among a multitude of daos. Affirming "the rightness of each thing as an expression of Nature without imposing your own biases" facilitates this equalization of all daos, including this one that equalizes them.

"Unite your heart with the silent vastness." There are some who deny that Zhuangzi advocated for any mystical experience at all, or that he was himself a mystic. This is in large part because they have correctly understood him as having eschewed all metaphysical knowledge. What they have failed to understand, however, is that this eschewal provides the very impetus for his mysticism. This is not what we traditionally understand as mysticism, where something 'out there' is experienced, but we needn't throw the baby out with the bathwater. "The silent void" is descriptive of our embedding in Mystery; uniting one's heart with 'this' is clearly a mystical experience in that it takes one beyond the rationalizing mind. It is, however, a purely psychological experience—no "void" is discovered.

The final story in this selection has Laozi explaining how an emperor should rule in a manner that perfectly sums up the teaching of the book that bears his name: "When an enlightened king rules his positive influence covers the entire world, but no one knows it comes from him. He transforms the world, yet no one depends on him. He remains unnamed, thus all the people are able to delight in themselves. He dwells in the unknowable and wanders where nothing in particular exists" (7:8). Rule by charisma allows people to find and follow their own paths in non-dependence. This is reminiscent of Shun's advice to Yao who wanted to dominate everyone: "Long ago ten suns rose in the sky and all things everywhere were brightly illuminated. How much better are multitudes of expressions of Dao than many suns" (2:47)!

REFLECTIONS—PART TWO

SPIRTUALITY IS NOT A PATH TO POWER

It is instructive in itself that the story of Liezi's pursuit of spirituality as a path to power was included here among those that address the exercise of political power (7:9). In the final analysis, what motivates the one motivates the other. We were told in the first chapter that Liezi could "ride the wind" (1:10), but Zhuangzi comments that although that helped him to avoid walking, because he was still dependent on "being somebody", it couldn't prove liberating. Though he appears last in a list of three progressively more 'enlightened' individuals, he still belongs to the same category as the politician. Here, we again encounter Liezi as someone who wants to master a dao so as to dominate others—to be someone—and is thus dominated by another. Those who wish to dominate others are unavoidably themselves dominated by others.

The various manifestations of Huzi's inner life offer a fertile field for speculative interpretation, but would probably draw us beyond what we can or need to know. His last manifestation explaining why the shaman fled does, however, address the real point of this story: "This time I showed him 'me' before I am 'me'—just an empty, chaotic impulse with no identifiable who or what. That's why he ran away" (7:17). The dao of Daoism is a path to the emptiness facilitated by the loss of one's 'me' and is as far removed from the pursuit of power as it is possible to be.

Liezi's final 'awakening' introduces a new and interesting twist to Zhuangzi's vision of sagacity: "He returned home . . . abandoning all 'spiritual' ambition, and allowing his carefully carved character to return to the uncarved block. Like a clod of earth, seemingly a chaos, he thus remained for the rest of his days" (7:18). We have already spoken of "the uncarved block", though it only appears here in the Inner Chapters. This is the Daoist metaphor for undifferentiated reality (Chaos) before humanity divides it up with self-consciousness and words. The experience of this is intended to inform our not-oneness, not to eliminate it. Becoming like a "clod of earth" echoes Shen Dao's reported exhortation (33): "Just become like an inanimate object. There is no need for sages or worthies. Indeed, a clump of earth never strays from the Dao" (Ziporyn; p 122). The author of this chapter approvingly (it seems) quotes Shen Dao's detractors: "The ambitious achievers would laugh at him saying, 'Shen Dao's dao is no practice for the living, but is a perfect guideline for the dead!'" If our experience of the uncarved block, chaos, were understood as eliminating the exercise of our not-oneness, then it would indeed be more appropriate for the dead than for the living. But such is not the case. If Liezi did in fact advocate for a kind of fatalistic monism, as some believe, then Zhuangzi clearly corrected him with his advocacy of walking two roads—the ability to simultaneously embrace oneness and our inescapable not-oneness.

Liezi's self-cultivation, his "carefully carved character", it turns out, was all an egoic exercise having nothing to do with true 'spirituality'. As Zhuangzi will shortly conclude: "Just be empty, nothing more."

JUST BE EMPTY

Zhuangzi sums it all up in two pithy verses (7:19, 20). In the first, we have: "Embody the endlessness" and "Just be empty, nothing more." Both suggest the loss of one's fixed-self, enabling the freedom to wander in the ever-changing. But Nature has given us a self, and this we can enjoy to the fullest. What Nature has not given us—guarantees of continuity, indisputable resolutions of our existential "dangle"—things that the religious mind hopes to gain—these, however, are not on offer. "Don't think you've gained anything thereby."

Being like a mirror, unmoved in one's innermost self by whatever events transpire—responding to them as they arise, letting them go as they pass—this is the mind of the sage. There is a sense in which this might be taken as suggesting a transcendent distancing from the world, and it is; but it is facilitated by a complete identification with and embracing of the world. And this is not accomplished in the abstract, but rather by fully affirming the very real and concrete vicissitudes of one's particular life experience. "Realizing that all lodgings are one, allow yourself to be lodged in whichever one cannot be avoided" (4:13). One remains "unmoved" by events, not through ignoring or denying them, but through fully embracing and accepting them.

A CREATION STORY

The concluding story of the Inner Chapters is, to my mind, one of the most poignant for its very simplicity (7:21). Chaos' two friends wish to repay him for his hospitality and thus give him the seven holes of humanity by which he can perceive the world as an experience of 'other'—the experience of not-oneness. "On the seventh day, Chaos died." I have called this a creation story because it reflects the birth of human consciousness and its sundering from the Whole. The book of Genesis has Adam and Eve eating of "the fruit of the knowledge of good and evil" and everything has been a mess since. But how would we know it was a mess without our being dualistic messes? Self-consciousness has its price, but as Zhuangzi says, "we delight in it nonetheless." Zhuangzi's entire project can be summed up as an attempt to find a way to reconnect with our undifferentiated, primal origin in Chaos so as to more fully enjoy our time 'outside' and differentiated from that origin. But how could he do this without making the same mistake as Chaos' friends who did not know how to help by not-helping? By creating a book of such jocular and fantastic ambiguity that whatever message we find there will be the one we discover for ourselves. Like his ruler mentioned above, through an eschewal of all "positive teachings" he leaves us to declare, "We did it all ourselves!" Such is the power of Zhuangzi's *Equalizing Jokebook* (1:2).

PART TWO

A PERSONAL PHILOSOPHY OF LIFE

CHAPTER EIGHT
THE SIMPLE WAY

IF I AM MISTAKEN

With respect to all that I have written here about the philosophy of Zhuangzi I may be completely mistaken. Yet, in the spirit of that philosophy as I have come to understand it, this matters little. It simply means that, like the forest trees responding to the Heavenly Belch, whatever sounds we make in response, we are all simply giving expression to our individuated human experiences, and that is all we can do, the best we can do. We are all together part of the Great Happening, and attempt to understand how we might best assume and affirm our places in that Happening, though every response can only be yet another expression of it.

I say that it matters 'little' because though it ultimately matters not at all, it can matter significantly in terms of our enjoyment of life. However momentary and inconsequential that may be, it is still the only true value to which human life seems to call us. That this enjoyment also requires and adds to the subsequent self-enjoyment of others with whom we interact similarly seems obvious.

Thus, if I have gotten Zhuangzi wrong, that needn't impact the value of my having read and interpreted him as I have. Perhaps this 'wrong' is 'right' for me. The proof of the pudding is in the eating.

There is, of course, the objective truth of what Zhuangzi said, or intended to say. But as we have so often said, a final definitive understanding of what this is must remain forever beyond our reach for a number of reasons. The most important of these, to my thinking, is that Zhuangzi intended that it be so. His ambiguity is by design. We are left to create our own daos by walking them—with the possible help of the sweep of his arm toward a panorama of vastness in an inviting gesture of welcome.

I have, of course, doubtless misread Zhuangzi in many instances. But there is only one controversial point of view that I have taken that I see as fundamental to whatever possible approximating understanding of his intended meanings we might achieve. I see this as one of those great interpretive forks in the road, the choice of which leads to radically different approaches to the project of life-enjoyment. If I am wrong on this, then I have misread Zhuangzi completely, and whatever benefit I might have accrued from grappling with his philosophy is purely accidental. This is my belief that Zhuangzi was completely innocent of all religious advocacy and practice. By this I mean that his way does not require that anything be true, and thus we are not called upon to commit ourselves to any particular belief or practice. There may be metaphysical Dao, but its existence or non-existence or transcendence of both has absolutely nothing to do with the realization of psychological Dao, the only vision to which, I believe, he aspired. The sage, no matter what name we might wish to give her, has simply realized a different way of seeing her place in the world. This experience may be profoundly mystical, but it is only so by virtue of its eschewal of any and every metaphysical belief. Zhuangzi's mysticism is innocent of all metaphysics. It depends on belief in nothing—not Dao, not *qi*, not Mind, not 'true nature'. It offers nothing outside the life experience as it manifests—not hope, not meaning, not purpose. If he practiced meditation or some other method of 'spiritual' practice, it was as a means to realizing this way of being in the world, not merging with anything outside of himself or the realization of any grand purpose or idealized self. Neither does this realization of psychological Dao in any way render one's apparently momentary existence more substantial. Nor is one in any way 'saved'—no need for salvation is ever considered. All is well, just as it is.

If I am wrong about this, I am thankfully so; for I can only follow an honest, non-religious path, one that requires no belief in propositional truth. If this means I am "punished by Heaven", then so be it—this too can be wandered in. If everything cannot be wandered in, then nothing can be wandered in, for wandering is dependent on nothing—indeed, it is this non-dependence.

THE SIMPLE WAY

I call my philosophy of life "The Simple Way". I call it *my* philosophy not because I see it as unique or independently derived, but because I am loathe to superimpose it upon the thought of anyone else. It is not strictly speaking the way of Zhuangzi if for no other reason than I cannot be entirely sure what that way is. Still, it is largely through my understanding of Zhuangzi and his interpreters that this perspective has arisen. In this sense, though certainly not strictly his philosophy, I see it as an honest adaptation of it as well as consistent with it.

In what sense is it "simple"? In the sense that it understands that absolutely nothing is required of us; all things are affirmed as they are, just as they are in any given moment. All is well. It is simple in that its realization is never other than in this very moment, as we are, however we are—it is contingent upon nothing, not even its realization—nothing must first be 'achieved', no merit accumulated, no insight into Truth acquired. We are, to our own minds, imperfect beings in need of improvement, or perhaps even salvation. Yet, though it seems obvious enough that as a species and as individuals we are indeed a moral and practical mess, in the end we are what Nature has wrought and thus, from that perspective, entirely affirmable—if indeed we are able to affirm Nature.

This, I believe, is in large part the message of Ziqi's forest trees. Though we would not likely declare a forest 'perfect', neither would we likely call it 'deficient' and in need of improvement. We affirm it because it is—as it is. Similarly, we affirm and appreciate every individual tree that makes up that forest. Though some may to our thinking be more beautiful than others by reason of their closer approximation to our ideal, still we recognize that each one has its own beauty simply by being the tree that it is. We also understand, moreover, that no ideal tree exists or ever will. Indeed, for all our discriminating preferences, we would be unlikely to judge any one tree as inferior to any other. So also might we affirm humanity and ourselves. This is the view from Dao, a view that transcends all moral and aesthetic distinctions in an equalizing affirmation, a view that shouts "Yes!" to all that is.

There is, of course, something apparently unique about humanity in that it tends to make these discriminations and is thus able to recognize its own deficiencies and those of its individual members. This, too, Nature has wrought. And thus this too is affirmable. And thus are we invited to walk two roads, to on the one hand recognize how all is well in being as it is, and on the other hand how we might improve ourselves and our collective expressions in that broader context.

Of these two, does one have priority over the other? Indeed, one does. Because humanity by default favors its own "characteristic human inclinations", it is necessary to emphasize that perspective that demonstrates the relative and contingent character of those inclinations. Were it otherwise, were it the case that humanity typically defaulted to the broader view that understands how that nothing it does ultimately matters, then it would be necessary to prioritize the perspective that understands how what we do *does* matter. It is very much as we saw with Yin and Yang paradigm. On the theoretical level they are equal and require no prioritization of one over the other. But from the perspective of self-conscious existence that is essentially a ceaseless yang-ing, it is necessary to prioritize Yin. Our relentless and fruitless pursuit of ultimate grounding leads to a debilitating disharmony with the givens of our existence, and this requires a prioritization of Yin, mystery, and a re-grounding in our groundlessness. The view from Dao, the ability to let "all things be illuminated by the light of a higher view" (2:18), is thus remedial.

Is the view from Dao a placebo, a view with no objectively demonstrable validity however effective? In view of our not-knowing, it is. But it is a placebo that is aware of itself as such and is yet all the more effective for that self-awareness. It remains, as every point of view must, completely within the realm of doubt. It is ever-self-effacing—it never takes itself too seriously.

The Simple Way, in recognizing no need to change, facilitates change, though it understands that no change was ever necessary. Thus, even when on a path of self-cultivation and growth, one is able always to affirm oneself just as one is.

NO CONDITIONS TO MEET

The Simple Way understands that, though there is a great deal we might do to improve our individual and collective experiences of being human, absolutely nothing we do affects ultimate outcomes. Nothing 'eternal' is at stake. If, as the Bible says, "all creation groaneth", this is not a consequence of a "Fall"—it is simply the way things have evolved and is thus devoid of moral implications. No salvation is required. All Is Well in the Great Mess. This is the ultimate background that informs all our doing and liberates us from the need to do anything at all.

This also implies that we are utterly affirmable just as we are. Any disenchantment about how we, others or the world might actually be is thus secondary and mediated. Wherever we might see ourselves on an imagined scale of achievement, 'spiritual' or otherwise, we are always unconditionally affirmable in precisely the same degree as we would be at any other position on that scale. This is the equalization of all things. We are perfect by virtue of our being perfectly who we are, however we are. This is the affirmation of not only ourselves, but of all that is.

The Buddha is represented as having said that the proof of his unsurpassable enlightenment was in that he gained absolutely *nothing* thereby. And though I agree with the sentiment that our bullshit meters should spike whenever we hear the oft repeated phrase "the Buddha said", still there is something profoundly liberating in this statement. Admittedly, it is probably meant in reference to some fantastic metaphysical belief regarding the nature of our being—that we are already Universal Mind, or something to that effect—but still, it is equally applicable in the context of a more mundane and phenomenological view of human experience. There is nothing we need do by way of self-improvement because relative to ultimate outcomes, nothing can or need be done. Whatever 'enlightenment' the Simple Way might facilitate, it is realized in realizing that no 'enlightenment' is necessary.

RELEASE IN TRUST

All the above, as long as it remains solely an intellectual assent, is but a prelude to what must ultimately be a 'mystical' movement if it is to facilitate the liberating freedom to wander. The concept of "hiding the world in the world" is intended as an opportunity for release into Reality, whatever that might ultimately 'be'. "Releasing the mind to play in all expressions"—this is Zhuangzi's simple suggestion of this movement.

Typically, 'mysticism' is understood as involving union with or the realization of some form of Ultimate Reality, but in Zhuangzi it is, as we have often said, utterly innocent of all knowing, and thus of all metaphysical presuppositions. "Ever not-knowing our own Source" speaks to our unavoidable interface with what I call Mystery. That the human psyche yearns for some form of grounding is self-evident. Yet, unless we are willing to put our faith in some imagined Ground, we are only left with the possibility of release into our own not-knowing. This I call release in trust.

This can also be understood as opening into Openness. Mystery is not a hidden 'thing', something 'there' that we are simply unable to perceive, but rather a sense (for it remains a purely human cognitive phenomenon) of empty openness without anything upon which to cognitively fix. The mystical movement of which I speak is of an opening into this Openness, a release into openness that requires that one also become an openness. This, I believe, is what Zhuangzi means by wandering. Yet we wander, not in nothingness, but in a world full of things, events and ideas. Openness implies and affirms the apparent existence of things and events, since these are the stuff of human experience, while allowing that none of them need be taken too seriously since within openness nothing is fixed and sure, nor need anything be so.

I have already suggested a distinction between "trust" and "faith". The latter implies something to believe in; "trust" is intended to suggest a release into what offers no propositional or explanatory truth at all. Faith is dependence upon some one thing; trust is a dependence upon everything without dependence on any one thing, and thus is a kind of non-dependence on anything. Faith mediates between the mind and the object of its faith. Trust is very much the act of living itself. To live is to trust. Release in trust is thus simply another way of saying, Live. Faith "adds to the process of life"—it has as its aim the addition of meaning and purpose which the life experience does not itself bestow. Trust is the affirmation of life itself, as it is, and to release oneself into it is to let life live oneself.

THANKFULNESS ARISES

All of this has but one aim—the fullest enjoyment of life. It is, as we have said, remedial; should there be anyone who experiences no such need, then it would itself simply be "adding to the process of life". However, the human condition appears to give rise naturally to a certain disharmony that leads us to seek some form of resolution. This disharmony is understood as entirely natural, a consequence of the evolution of human self-awareness—not a great Fall from grace, however imagined. No need for a cosmic redemption is envisioned or implied.

The aim, then, is to feel good. And thankfulness is, in this author's experience, just such a feeling. Yet, just as the entire Zhuangzian vision cannot be prescribed and still be consistent with itself, so also—and doubly so—an individual experience of that vision approximately realized cannot be prescribed. Thus, I offer thankfulness as only an anecdotal example of a positive outcome of Zhuangzian wandering.

Thankfulness arises. Thankfulness happens consequent to releasing oneself in trust into Openness. Thankfulness spontaneously arises. And among its attributes is joy.

We do not say, Be thankful. That would be prescriptive, mediated, doing—and ineffective. Thankfulness, like the pleasure of play, is genuine only when it arises without intention.

SO WHAT?!

The (fictional) sage Zhouzi passed two of his disciples arguing in the courtyard. When he asked what the problem was, one declared that the other had called him a "blockhead". "You're both blockheads!" retorted Zhouzi as he continued on his way. But then, speaking over his shoulder he said, "And so am I. So what?!"

Zhouzi's simple "So what?" encapsulates the entirety of his teaching that there are indeed no conditions to meet. He taught the Simple Way. What are the ultimate outcomes of him and his disciples being "blockheads"? None. In the vastest arrangement everything is a wash. All is well. Should we wish to discriminate between levels of moral or 'spiritual' attainment, thinking of some people as saints and sages however, to the extent that we are capable of true honesty, we will be sorely disappointed. There are no sages—if by sages we mean "perfected" beings. There may be a place for positing theoretical sages as a means to facilitating an approximating realization of the attributes they are imagined to embody, but the moment we actually believe in any such possibility we set ourselves on a trajectory of vain, fixated and religious striving. We become dependent on an idea—and one can only wander in the "harmony of all *de*", not in the fixated pursuit of only one. Should we actually believe we have discovered a "perfected" sage, then unless we are capable of serious self-deception our faith will ultimately be shattered. Human beings are by nature 'imperfect' and no amount of wishful thinking will make it otherwise. Zhuangzian liberation is had in this realization, not in the pursuit of what is unattainable.

Zhouzi simply realized that he was perfect by virtue of being perfectly who he was, however imperfect that might be.

"So what?" speaks to horizontal relationships as well as to the vertical relationship of ultimate outcomes. Someone calls me a blockhead. So what? The exploration of this question reaches to the depth of the practical outcomes of the Simple Way. Why does this bother me? Because there is a 'me' to be bothered. Because if true, my 'worthiness' is diminished. Why do I wish to strike back and declare my critic 'wrong'?

Because I dwell in the realm of right and wrong. Why do I believe it's my job to tell my critic that he is 'wrong' and needs to change? Because I dwell in the realm of right and wrong and thus cannot not-be the change, but instead must impose my opinions on others.

It may be thought that the realization that there are no conditions to meet, that one is perfect in being perfectly who one is, somehow allows one to escape all responsibility for one's actions and responses; quite the contrary—release from the default "characteristic human inclinations" puts the onus of responsibility squarely on the individual in such a way that no one or no thing ever shares that responsibility. Responsible for every response, where is there ever room for blame?

A CLOSING 'UNSPIRITUAL' POSTSCRIPT

Needless to say, nothing I have said here is true. It is not true of the world. Nor of Zhuangzi. Nor of myself. It is but an interpretation of a dream within a dream, and its only value is in the possibility of its furthering the enjoyment of my life. But it has already accomplished that—not as the realization of a goal—sagacity—but as a consequence of the formulating of one. "Daos are formed by walking them" we are told; and it is in the walking that our daos have meaning. It is not in the realization of the goals of a philosophy of life that its primary value is found, but in the act of creating that philosophy. Thus, while we disagree with the discriminating assumption of the Socratic pronouncement that "The unexamined life is not worth living", still we agree that a life examined is a life more likely to be enjoyed. Again, this is remedial; were we born sages, no such self-examination would be necessary or contemplated. Our bias toward intellectual complexity and in-depth inquiry is consequent to our having arrived at the need for the same. Yet it seems likely that the life-enjoyment of a simple farmer plowing behind his camel in rural Rajasthan might very well exceed that of those who require the formulation of elaborate philosophies. In any case, if any life is worth living, then every life is worth living. And from the Zhuangzian perspective, the only known 'value' of life is in its enjoyment.

BIBLIOGRAPHY

Ames, Roger, ed. *Wandering at Ease in the* Zhuangzi. Albany: State University of New York Press, 1998.

Carr, Karen L., and Ivanhoe, Philip J. *The Sense of Antirationalism: The Religious Thought of Zhuangzi and Kierkegaard.* Seven Bridges, 2000.

Chan, Wing-tsit. *A Source Book in Chinese Philosophy.* Princeton: Princeton University Press, 1963.

Clark, Richard B. trans. *Hsin Hsin Ming.* Buffalo: White Pines Press, 1973.

Cleary, Thomas. *The Taoist Classics.* 4 vol. Boston: Shambhala, 1999.

____. *The Way of the World: Readings in Chinese Philosophy.* Boston: Shambhala, 2009.

Cook, Scott, ed. *Hiding the World in the World: Uneven Discourses on the* Zhuangzi. Albany: State University of New York Press, 2003.

Coutinho, Steve. *An Introduction to Daoist Philosophies.* New York: Columbia University Press, 2014.

De Bary, William Theodore, et al. *Sources of Chinese Tradition* Vol. 2. New York: Columbia University Press, 1960.

Fung Yulan. *A Short History of Chinese Philosophy.* trans. Derk Bodde. New York: Macmillan, 1948.

____. *A History of Chinese Philosophy*, trans. Derk Bodde. Vol. 1. Princeton: Princeton University Press, 1953.

____. *Chuang-tzu: A New Selected Translation with an Exposition of the Philosophy of Kuo Hsiang*. New York: Paragon Books, 1964.

Ge Ling Shang. *Liberation as Affirmation: The Religiosity of Zhuangzi and Nietzsche*. Albany: State University of New York Press, 2006.

Graham, A. C. *Chuang Tzu: The Seven Inner Chapters and Other Writings from the Book of Chuang-Tzu*. London: Allen and Unwin, 1981.

____. *Disputers of the Tao: Philosophical Argument in Ancient China*. La Salle, IL: Open Court, 1989.

Hansen, Chad. *A Daoist Theory of Chinese Thought: A Philosophical Interpretation*. New York: Oxford University Press, 1992.

Kaltenmark, Max. *Lao Tzu and Taoism*. Stanford: Stanford University Press, 1969.

Kjellberg, Paul, and P. J. Ivanhoe, eds. *Essays on Skepticism, Relativism, and Ethics in the Zhuangzi*. Albany: State University of New York Press, 1996.

Kohn, Livia. *Zhuangzi: Text and Context*. Dunedin, FL: Three Pines Press, 2014.

Lau. L. M., trans. *Tao Te Ching*. Harmondsworth: Penguin Books, 1963.

Liu, Xiaogan. *Classifying the Zhuangzi Chapters*. trans., William E. Savage. Anne Arbor: University of Michigan, 1994.

Mair, Victor H., tans. *Wandering on the Way: Early Taoist Tales and Parables of Chuang-Tzu*. Honolulu: University of Hawai'i Press, 1994.

____. ed. *Experimental Essays on Chuang-tzu*. Dunedin, FL: Three Pines, 2010.

Merton, Thomas. *The Way of Chuang Tzu*. New York: New Directions, 1969.

Munro, Donald J. *The Concept of Man in Early China*. Stanford: Stanford University Press, 1969.

Palmer, Martin. *The Book of Chuang-tzu*. London: Penguin, 1996.

Waley, Arthur. trans., *The Analects of Confucius: Translated and Annotated by Arthur Waley*. New York: Vintage, 1938.

____. *The Way and Its Power: A Study of the* Tao De Ching *and Its Place in Chinese Thought*. London: Allen and Unwin, 1934.

Wang Bo. *Zhuangzi: Thinking Through the Inner Chapters*. Livia Kohn, trans. St. Petersburg, FL, 2014.

Watson, Burton. *The Complete Works of Chuang Tzu*. New York: Columbia University Press, 1968.

Wu Kuang-Ming. *Chuang Tzu: World Philosopher at Play*. New York: Crossroad, 1982.

____. *The Butterfly as Companion: Meditations on the First Three Chapters of the* Chuang Tzu. Albany: State University of New York Press, 1990.

Ziporyn, Brook. *The Penumbra Unbound: The Neo-Daoist Philosophy of Guo Xiang*. Albany: State University of New York Press, 2003.

____, trans. *Zhuangzi: The Essential Writings with Selections from Traditional Commentaries*. Indianapolis: Hackett Publishing, 2009.

____. *Ironies of Oneness and Difference: Coherence in Early Chinese Thought; Prolegomena to the Study of* Li. Albany: State University of New York Press, 2012.

____. *Beyond Oneness and Difference:* Li *and Coherence in Chinese Buddhist Thought and Its Antecedents*. Albany: State University of New York Press, 2013.